CHRISTIANS AND THE THIRD WORLD

Christians and the Third World

David W. Edgington

Exeter
The Paternoster Press

AUSTRALIA
Bookhouse Australia Ltd
P.O. Box 115, Fremington Markets,
N.S.W. 2129

SOUTH AFRICA
Oxford University Press
P.O. Box 1141,
Cape Town

British Library Cataloguing in Publication Data

Edgington, David W.
   Christians and the Third World.
   1. Underdeveloped areas—Missions—History
   I. Title
   266'.009172'4   BV2470

ISBN 0-85364-286-9

Typeset by Nuprint Services Limited, Harpenden and printed and bound in Great Britain at The Pitman Press, Bath for The Paternoster House, 3 Mount Radford Crescent, Exeter, Devon.

Contents

ACKNOWLEDGEMENTS

This book owes a considerable debt to many people who have helped in a number of ways. I am grateful for the guidance of Richard Jolly, Director of the Institute of Development Studies, Sussex, in presenting some of the material in Chapter 2; to Rev. A. Clements and to Dr and Mrs A. Hopkins (BMS), Rev. Canon S. Barrington-Ward (CMS), Mr G. W. Dearsley (SUM), Nigel Sylvester (SU International), Mr Arthur Pont (BMMF), Mr Dennis Smith (EUSA), Mr T. P. Hunt (RBMU) and to representatives of Tear Fund for allowing me to interview them; to Rev. Theodore Williams of the Evangelical Fellowship of India and to John Howell of the Lausanne Committee for World Evangelization, Nairobi, for their useful inputs in Chapter 4, and also to Peter Cotterell, Director of Overseas Studies at London Bible College and to Ernest Oliver, founder secretary of the EMA, for their invaluable advice on a number of occasions. My thanks are also due to Jenny for her useful criticisms at draft stage, to Pat for coping so admirably with my hieroglyphics, and to Judy for her unfailing support and understanding when her husband was miles away when spoken to!

1

Is it any of our business?

Is it necessary to write a book about the Christian's responsibility to the Third World? Is the title not perhaps rather misleading, disguising what may turn out to be only another appeal for greater missionary interest, and in particular, for more generous financial support?

In point of fact, this is not a 'missionary' book in the accepted sense, although clearly some sections will be devoted to a critique of past missionary strategy and others will describe church growth in parts of the world which were traditionally 'missionary' areas. It is rather an attempt to update the Christian's thinking about, and perhaps more important, his attitudes towards, people and places in what is becoming generally known as the Third World – Africa, Asia, Latin America and the Caribbean.

But shouldn't we concentrate first of all on putting our own house in order? A recent survey of church growth in the United Kingdom indicated that the 'main line' churches have all suffered from a decline in members. Since 1970 there has been a decline of 2.8% in the Episcopal churches, of 2.7% in the Baptist churches, and the decline in Methodist, United Reformed and Catholic churches is 1.9%, 1.9% and 0.7% respectively. Total membership (in absolute numbers) has declined from 7,879,000 to 7,275,000. Similarly the number of ministers has declined by over 2,000. Although statistics like these cannot tell us anything about the spiritual state of the churches, they do point out in stark terms that numerically the church in this country is contracting, and the same evidence indicates that young people aren't being attracted to the church in the numbers they were 20 years ago. In any case, most of us don't really need these statistics to remind us of the unhealthy state of the church in Britain today, particularly in the inner city areas – the evidence is unfortunately too obvious. A drive through the inner city areas of London, of Birmingham or Manchester will reveal empty churches, used either as furniture depositories or ripe for demolition. It wouldn't be so bad if our drive could be continued for a few miles and revealed scores of purpose-built churches in the new housing estates, with every evidence of constant use and acting as spearheads into homes completely untouched by the Gospel – but this is just not the case. Of course there are many examples of thriving churches, and indeed a few of these are in inner city areas, but the fact remains that by and large we in England are not living in a period of exciting church growth.

Nor are we living in a Christian Britain today in terms of morals, industrial ethics or marital standards. The ongoing industrial strife of which we are all aware has many causes, but one of them is certainly human greed; we are constantly being reminded of the soaring divorce rate and of all the attendant human scarring that is caused by the breakup of a family unit; we cannot fail to be conscious that violence between one group of men and another has become so commonplace that its monotonous appearance on our television screens at nine o'clock elicits virtually no emotional response from many of us.

So why a book on the Third World? Is our need not for more books suggesting ways in which the Gospel can make a greater impact on *our own society?* Isn't there a very real risk that any book about the Third World will degenerate into another rather dreary book on politics and men's ideas, rather than a Word from the Lord? Isn't it dangerous to write about politics and economics, to ask why some countries are so poor while others get richer; to investigate the reasons underlying the hatred between black and white in Southern Africa today? Readers representing different social or political viewpoints are likely to take up their entrenched positions and the last state might well be worse than the first! Shouldn't we leave these vexed questions to the politicians, and concentrate rather on becoming more effective witnesses, as we surrender to the leading of the Holy Spirit? If 'all our doings "were" ordered by His governance', if we were walking openly with the Lord, then surely the problems of tensions between the different ethnic groups and of inequalities in society would quickly disappear, and we would find that men and women of different cultural backgrounds and ethnic groups would learn to live together in harmony, all acknowledging the Unity of the Church of Jesus Christ?

If the sentiments expressed in this last sentence were true, then there would most certainly be no need to write this book. But they are not; the Church in this country is generally cosy and inward-looking, unaware of and insensitive towards the problems and aspirations of the Third World. Christians are (in general) content to give to missionary societies, organise the occasional missionary meeting when Bryan and Joyce (who were brought up in the Sunday School anyway) come home from Onga-Bonga with their slides, and make a little extra effort for Christian Aid week. They look the other way when they learn that yet another black church has been founded in Victorian downtown; they regard the news that a Sikh gurdwara has been established in the now forsaken building of the local Presbyterian church as yet another reminder of our present pagan society, now aggravated by the growth of other, non-Christians, religious groups in that society. Some Christian leaders would go so far as to oppose this kind of redeployment of church buildings, on the ground that they were originally consecrated for Christian worship, and to use them for the worship of 'other gods' amounts to desecration.

This book is intended to provide a clearer understanding, not only of the realities of the contemporary Third World, but also of some of the complexities and challenges of living in a multi-cultural society here in Britain. And better understanding can follow only a more informed awareness of the way different people think and behave. When Jesus commissioned the first missionaries 'to evangelise all nations' (Matt. 28:19-20) he will have expected them to take the trouble to know something about their culture and way of life in order to be able to understand them more fully. For he was himself always sensitive to the peculiar needs of individuals. He surprised the Samaritan woman and compelled her to listen to what he had to say because he knew so much about her different religious emphases, as well as her own personal situation (John 4:8-25). He recognised the authority of the Roman Centurion (Luke 7:2-10), and the intellectual difficulties facing the Jewish religious leader Nicodemus. One of his most widely-travelled followers was determined to become like a Jew in order to win Jews, yet also to become like a Gentile in order to win them. He was, indeed, prepared to become everything in turn to men of every sort so that he might save some (1 Cor. 9:20-22).

Today we need to follow Paul's example. If we are to pray

intelligently for missionaries, we need to know much more about the society in which they work – which is probably a lot more complex than we'd realised! We need to know, for example, that they are neither alien administrators nor in the pay of the British church, but rather servants of the new national church. We may be surprised to discover that their Director is an African, educated at London Bible College and determined to sweep away those elements in the church that to him smack of Western Imperialism – including *Hymns Ancient and Modern!*

Perhaps even more important, we need to realise how one-sided is the old exotic image of African society that still clings tenaciously to many Christian memories. We may be surprised to learn, for example, that West Africa contains three towns with a population as large as the entire urban area of Manchester, and a further ten larger than Southampton. Lagos, a city of well over 1½ million people, has its own coloured television network, and Nigeria boasts 13 universities. Ghana has a further three. Primitive countries still exist in the Third World – indeed for many millions of people Western innovations scarcely impinge at all upon their way of life, but we would have a very distorted view of the Third World if our only image is one of backwardness.

So we need to know more about 'them' if we are to communicate with them more effectively – and perhaps we have already come to appreciate that effective evangelisation must mean more than merely shouting the Gospel at people from the pulpits of half-empty churches.

One could well argue, on the other hand, that we suffer from having *too much,* not *too little,* information. The mass media are constantly focusing on the Third World. We are reminded that we are living in a 'global village', and, thanks to our television networks, we can travel round the world quite comfortably, merely sitting in our lounges. Whether we choose to enjoy the slightly exotic image presented by programmes such as *Whicker's World* or take a more serious look through the films of Felix Greene or the various *Panorama* programmes, the world is rapidly shrinking and 'we' and 'they' are being brought much closer together. Of course, a good many readers will have travelled to the Third World on business or for a holiday; it's only 7½ hours flying time to Accra or 15½hours to Bombay. When my family first travelled to East Africa in 1961, we travelled by boat and it took us nearly three weeks, but in 1982 I can leave London after an evening meal and have breakfast in Nairobi the next morning.

If our world is shrinking in terms of travel time, contemporary trade patterns remind us even more powerfully of the nearness of the Third World, and of the growing interdependence between the Third World and the West. We shall not easily forget the impact of the sudden rise in oil prices in 1973-74, and other commodities produced in the Third World have caused similar startling increases to our overall cost of living. British Rail coffee is quite a luxury at 28p a cup! Whether we like it or not, the West is finding that its economic livelihood is increasingly bound up with the Third World, and nowadays we can no longer exploit Third World producers as we might have done fifty years ago.

The trouble is that in spite of all the information they offer, the media aren't particularly concerned to present a *balanced* picture of the Third World. Their role is not to educate as much as to provide us with news-worthy items – or sometimes just titbits. Racial riots in South Africa, yes; the latest outburst by an African politician at the United Nations Assembly, yes: floods in India or earthquakes in Iran, yes; another bloody coup in South America, yes; – but what about the good news? The 20th General Conference of UNESCO (March 1978) saw the role of the media as sufficiently important to pass a declaration, recognising the important contribution the media make both in strengthening peace and international understanding, and in educating young people in a spirit of justice. Third World journalists have understandably become concerned for the impression of their countries presented by Western newspapers, and sought to improve this crisis – loaded image. As the BBC commentator reporting this item said, most of us had probably never heard of Guyana until we were told of the People's Temple commune massacres in that country, and although the bizarre happenings there had nothing to do with Guyana, many people would henceforth always associate the country with lawlessness. Most of us form our images of the Third World from the stories presented by the media – no wonder we end up with an horrific picture of an Africa that is permanently in political turmoil, or an India that lurches from one flood to another drought.

Of course most Third World countries have experienced various difficulties as they struggle to establish themselves on the diplomatic chessboard, but it would do us no harm to remember that quite a number of these difficulties have their roots deep in history, and were often exacerbated by the rapaciousness of European colonial enterprises 100 years ago. Even so, we need to get a balanced overview of what is happening in the Third World, rather than allow ourselves to be satiated by an over-abundance of bad news, or at least news that conveys an impression of constant turbulence and distress. As we shall discover in Chapter 2, some Third World countries can tell stories of economic and educational development and of originality in using their resources that indicate a high level of national integrity and industriousness. It is important to 'refocus' our image of the Third World, then, in order to gain an understanding beyond the newsworthy snippets meted out to us by the media.

But we don't need to rely solely on what the media tell us about events on the other side of the world. For the Third World has come to live in Britain! There are approximately 2 million people living in Britain who were either themselves born in a Third World country or whose parents were born there, and these are people whom we meet daily.[2] It is not the main purpose of this book to discuss the complex issue of race relations in Britain today, but recent disturbances in many inner-city areas make it abundantly plain that they are far from satisfactory. What is perhaps more tragic is the fact that the Church has done very little towards improving understanding between the various ethnic minorities in Britain. By and large the Church, comfortably surburban and middle-class (and thus already distanced from the problems), ignores the issues involved. It is easier to support its missionaries 3,000 miles away, and to ignore the fact that those same people to whom they have been sending missionaries for the past century have now come to live just round the corner. Too often the churches in the inner city areas, where the population is most multi-ethnic, are themselves struggling to survive, and the more prosperous churches are either too busy fostering their own schemes to be aware of the need to look carefully at the biblical approach to race, or else prefer to mark the subject 'too hot to handle', and leave well alone! If involvement in the issue of community relations means the risk of taking political stances and sides they prefer to hold back. 'Political' involvement might alienate certain church members (perhaps influential and even wealthy ones), so the issue tends to be avoided in the interests of peace within the body.

Similarly, there is a fear of being involved in 'interfaith' dialogue. A number of multi-ethnic areas have seen positive moves towards a sharing of religious experience in the hope that all may thus get a little nearer to the truth. In Birmingham, for example, the Interfaith Council seeks to function as a forum where members of the different faiths can meet together in mutual respect and confidence and promote fuller understanding. This group addressed itself to the question of Religious Education in schools and as a result an Agreed Syllabus has been adopted which is not distinctly Christian in its emphasis.

'Interfaith' is certainly a vexed issue, and readers can do no better than to read Maurice Hobbes's chapter in *Jesus Christ _ the Only Way* (ed. P. Sookhdeo, Exeter, 1978). It is right for Christians to believe in the uniqueness of the Christian revelation, and to proclaim that there is no other Name given under Heaven whereby we can be saved (Acts 4:12). All the same – Jesus must have shocked his listeners by telling them the story of the Good Samaritan! The Priest and Levite, for all their religious correctness, failed at the point of real individual need; the Samaritan, a man of mixed race and unorthodox faith, succeeded. To the question 'Who is my neighbour?' the lawyer's answer was clear: 'The one who showed mercy.' Jesus was not advocating that his Jewish listeners become Samaritans; but he *was* publicly expressing approval of the Samaritan's love in action. Is there a lesson here for Christians today vis-a-vis our understanding of the culture of our Hindu or Muslim neighbours?

What then should be the approach of the Christian to members of other ethnic groups living in his town? It would be easy to isolate 'race' as a topic always associated with violence, instability, riots, and so forth, yet this ignores the positive aspects of a multi-racial society. Nor should we allow ourselves to become paternalistic in trying to adopt special attitudes towards other groups. One basic issue for Christians in a multi racial society is that in our overall pattern of church growth we must discover ways to avoid the development of 'black' and 'white' churches in this country – and this may well mean abandoning some of our long-established habits of worship, and welcoming, for example, a more spontaneous form if this will help to bring black and white churches together. It will also mean spending much more time learning about the culture and domestic backgrounds of the ethnic minorities living in our town, so that we can have some point of contact. Merely to state lamely that they won't speak to us won't do! Jesus usually took the initiative when he met people. He made the first move and quite startled the Samaritan woman at the well (John 4:7-17), and his initiative to Zacchaeus nearly caused him to fall out of his tree!

But we can't begin to communicate with people until we know something about them. Missionary societies still send their young candidates to a Bible College where at least part of the curriculum involves some understanding of the culture of the people with whom they are going to live. It wasn't until Hudson Taylor realised the importance of living side by side with the Chinese people and even dressing like them that he was able to gain their confidence. More recently, Elizabeth Elliott, widow of Jim (*Through Gates of Splendour*) went back to live with the Auca people in Peru. Humanly speaking, it was her willingness totally to identify with them that has been responsible for the subsequent birth of an Auca church.

Although the parallels suggested above aren't exact, in that men and women from the Third World have come to live with us rather than our going to live with them, the lesson is obvious. The more we understand about Indian family life, for example, the more likely it is that we shall be able to build bridges of friendship with our Indian neighbours. The more we know of the black experience and some of the reasons why West Indians living in Britain are so often angry and disillusioned, the more likely it is that black and white communities can begin to share their experiences, and in Christ learn to forgive and to accept his Lordship, as they worship together.

There is one final, and very cogent, reason why we should be stimulated into thinking more carefully about the Third World. That is because very many of those who live in Third World countries are poor, and need the help of caring Christian people. A fuller consideration of the extent of, and some of the reasons for, this poverty follows in the next chapter, but readers must know something of the poverty in the Third World through the information supplied by agencies such as Christian Aid and Tear Fund. The fact, for example, that in developing countries one child in four dies before the age of five, whereas in developed countries less than one in fifty dies before reaching school; or that some countries have only one doctor per 70,000 people may help us to appreciate the grim meaning of poverty.

Mr and Mrs Alarin and their five children live in an eight by ten foot room in the Philippines. He is an ice vendor; she makes a coconut sweet which she sells on the street, and reckons to make 25 pence a month. She said to a missionary visitor recently:

> I feel so sad when my children cry at night because they have no food. I know my life will never change. What can I do to solve my problems? I

am so worried about the future of my children. I want them to go to school but how can we afford it? I am sick most of the time, but I can't go to the doctor because each visit costs fifteen pence and the medicine is extra. What can I do?[3]

When Jesus saw the crowds hungry he turned to his disciples and said: 'You give them something to eat!' (Matthew 14:16.) It is all too easy to spiritualize the parables of Jesus, and certainly they do have a spiritual dimension. But on this occasion Jesus was aware of men's physical needs and told his disciples to satisfy that need. Indeed, he quickly identified with the Servant of Isaiah who had come to free the oppressed and heal the sick (Luke 4:18 & 19).

That commission hasn't been revoked. The Christian gospel demands that we care for the *whole* man, not just his soul. And this will mean caring for our hungry fellow-men, and perhaps showing a particular care for our fellow-believers in the Third World, as we gain insight into their condition.

The following chapters offer some background information about the Third World. They are not intended to read like extracts from a geography textbook, nor indeed from a political survey. Rather the book has been written for all who are anxious to be better informed about God's world and want to equip themselves better to share their faith – which also implies sharing time and resources – with others. This survey will certainly enable us to reappraise long-accepted mission strategies, and to share in the excitement of a phase in church growth unprecedented in any other period of history, as churches in the Third World multiply, not only in numbers, but in terms of maturity and spiritual experience. It may even bring us to pray with a greater sense of urgency for those Sikhs in the Presbyterian Church down the road.

2

The Third World in the eighties

The phase 'The Third World' has now become well accepted by common usage, but it would be useful to reach a meaningful definition. It was first used in Paris in 1956, when a French writer suggested that there was a close parallel between Le Tiers Monde (Third World) and Le Tiers État (The Third Estate) in revolutionary France. More recently, the phrase is used in the context of the post-war power blocks: the Western, basically capitalist block, comprising Western Europe, America and Canada, Australia and New Zealand: the Eastern block, comprising the Communist countries in Eastern Europe and the USSR: and the Third World, consisting of those countries that are, at least in principle, politically uncommitted. The same countries are, by and large, economically poor, educationally underprivileged and still in a state of development, but it would be incorrect to stereotype them all as 'poor' and 'backward' – they offer a very wide variety of economic and cultural backgrounds.

Drawing up a list of countries of the Third World is therefore a rather arbitrary business, with a number of countries very difficult to classify. The present United Nations list comprises:

ALL ASIA	(except Japan, mainland China, Mongolia, North Korea, North Vietnam and Asian parts of the USSR)
ALL AFRICA	(except the Republic of South Africa)
THE CARIBBEAN	
CENTRAL AMERICA	
SOUTH AMERICA	

18

OCEANIA   (except Australia and New
                                 Zealand)
MALTA, GIBRALTAR and CYPRUS

It should again be pointed out, however, that this list should not
be regarded as sacrosanct, and a number of countries remain
very difficult to classify. The oil-rich countries of the Middle East
are technically part of the Third World, and indeed many of the
ordinary people's life style has not changed from a very simple
rural existence, yet four of these countries are in the 'Top League'
of countries with the highest per capita income in the world. The
writer would have included Mongolia, Korea and Vietnam on
his list and omitted Malta, Gibraltar and Cyprus.

THE COMPLEXITY OF THE THIRD WORLD

Although it would be presumptuous and thoroughly misleading
to lump all Third World countries together and write blandly of
Third World characteristics, there are nevertheless some broad
generalisations that can properly be made. It may be helpful
briefly to list some of these characteristics at this stage in the
chapter and then to comment fully on some of them later on.
Politically, nearly all of them have become independent, either
since the end of World War II, or, in the case of the South
American countries, much earlier. Thus they are all going through
the problems of finding their feet and discovering the way in
which they wish to develop. They do not owe political allegiance
to either West or East, but instead jealously guard their newly
won independence and assert, sometimes rather aggressively, a
policy of non-allegiance. Most, but not all, countries in the Third
World are poor. Perhaps poverty is the one characteristic that
most people identify with the Third World, and they have come
almost to *expect* to be confronted by a Christian Aid collecting
box or envelope. This can indeed be misleading, in that the
words 'poor' and 'poverty' need careful definition if they are to
have any meaning. Do we include only cash or property assets,
for example, when assessing a person's wealth, or also his subsistence – style farm? Western economists are not able to assess
the latter in cash terms, so subsistence figures cannot show on
the tables or enter into the calculations used in this chapter.
    Before we go on to consider the meanings of 'poverty', 'wealth'
and 'development' purely in economic terms, however, it would

be as well to remind ourselves that *development* implies *change*, and change in other directions than merely in living standards. A country that has a developed sense of national justice or of social responsibility, albeit with a low per capita income, may be further along the road to national development than another country that has a high per capita income but also a high crime rate and little care for its senior citizens. Are there any biblical guidelines to help us in our search for a pattern of national development pleasing to God?

This very important issue is considered further in Chapter 5 but readers may like to refer to an excellent article in *Third Way* (March '79, Vol. 3, No. 3) by Erica Wheeler – 'Every Country a Developing Country'.

The usual method of measuring a nation's wealth, (and thus comparing one country with another) is to use the GNP (Gross National Product) and *per-capita income*, and by drawing up a table of comparisons to put countries in certain categories of poverty or wealth. The trouble is that this alone tells us nothing about the *distribution* of wealth in a given country (which is usually more uneven in Third World countries than in the West), nor does it allow for the large degree of subsistence farming that is common to many of them. Even more significantly, it tells nothing about the purchasing power of that income – and in some countries in the Third World, inflation is running extremely high. But having made all these provisos, the figures are shattering, as Table 1 shows.

Table 1
GNP (Gross National Product), Per Capita Income 1978, and Average Annual Growth Rate 1960–70 and 1970–78 (%) of Selected Countries

Country	GNP £ million sterling	Per Capita Income £	% Growth Rate (a) 1960–1970	(b) 1970–1978
Ethiopia	1,435	55	+1.9	−0.1
Bangladesh	3,640	45	−0.4	+0.2
Nepal	790	60	+0.2	+0.3
Nigeria	24,050	300	+3.5	+4.4
Sri Lanka	1,435	100	+1.1	+1.9
Tanzania	2,065	120	+2.6	+1.7
Zaïre	3,240	120	+1.4	−2.2
U.K.	159,740	2,860	+2.7	+1.9
Switzerland	40,965	6,490	+2.3	+0.0

N.B. There are 36 countries, with an overall population of 2,008 million with a per capita income of less than £150 per annum, and a further 31 countries, with an overall population of 493 million, with a per capita income of between £150–£300 per annum. Of the 25 countries with a per capita income of over £3,000 per annum, 14 are in Europe and four are rich oil-producing countries (Kuwait, Libya, Qatar and the United Arab Eminates). The other seven are the Faeroe Islands, Brunei, Japan, Australia, American Samoa, Canada and Bermuda.

(Source: World Bank Report 1980)

These and other statistics will help us to gain an analytical and statistical understanding of poverty, and make us appreciate the enormous gulf between our standard of living and that accepted by some Third World countries. But perhaps the following personal observations will make the picture much more graphic. Arthur Hopcraft in his book *Born to Hunger* describes his personal reaction to poverty in a poor part of a Brazilian town:

> Inevitably there was no sanitation. Around the shacks was strewn the rubbish of the destitute, and a thick layer of it covered the sides of the culvert all the way down to the grey-green slime at the bottom. It was dry weather. After rain that spot would reek abominably. The people were pitifully ragged: a mis-shapen old woman in a filthy dress, old men shrivelled by sun and sickness, and a crowd of sickly children showing all the signs of neglect and poor feeding... the boys had the round pot bellies of malnutrition.

Another factor common to nearly all Third World countries is their *rapid population growth*. Largely because of recent medical preventive techniques, the infant mortality rate has dropped sharply, and for reasons which will be considered later, birth control in the Third World has not yet been totally accepted. Thus the annual population growth in the UK and in West Germany in the '70s has been 0.1%; yet in Nigeria it is 2.6% and in Mexico 3.3%. The world figure is 1.9% and nearly all Third World countries have a growth rate higher than that. 75% of the world's population is living in the Third World – three out of every four people living in the world today. India's growth rate (2.1%) is not in fact as high as some other countries in the Third World, but in common with a number of other countries in the Third World, her problem is that, even with a growth rate of 2.1%, the population of India is increased by some 15,000,000 annually. It is all too easy for a 'tread mill' situation to emerge, whereby increased production of food achieved by improved technical or scientific methods is merely swallowed up by the extra mouths that have to be fed.

Nearly all Third World countries rely largely on *agriculture* for their major source of income. We need to rid ourselves of the image of the prosperous English farmer enjoying a comfortable standard of living in a very healthy rural setting, and think rather of a peasant farmer either growing just enough food to support himself and his family, or growing a single primary product which is subject to enormous price fluctuations on the world market. In fact 90% of the export earnings of the developing countries derive from primary products, and in many cases countries depend on a single commodity for over half of their export earnings, as Table 2 shows.

Table 2
Third World dependence upon Single Commodities

Country	Commodity	% of all exports
Sri Lanka	Tea	55
Ghana	Cocoa	65
Cuba	Sugar	84
Zambia	Copper	94
Gambia	Groundnuts	85

N.B. The price of Zambian copper dropped from £1,500 to £645 per ton within one year, 1974. But the price of imports to Zambia continued to rise in that same year, so that the volume of imports Zambia's export earnings could buy fell by 45%.

(Source: North-South – a Programme for Survival)

Although both the West and the Eastern blocs do buy these (and other) primary products, the price they command on the world markets varies enormously from one year to the next. Even more seriously, the demand for one particular product can virtually disappear overnight if a cheaper substitute is marketed. When I first went to Tanzania in 1962, sisal (used in manufacturing sacks or coarse carpeting) was £145 a ton, and this enabled sisal farmers to employ an appreciable number of African labourers, and – at least in theory – to provide a minimal wage and a few amenities for them. When I returned to visit Tanzania in 1968, the demand for sisal had virtually disappeared, as nylon and paper replaced it in manufacturing sacks and string. I remember driving through miles of uncut sisal, because it was not worth paying even rock bottom wages to harvest it. But what about the African labourers whose livelihood had come from that task? Where as a worker in this country who has, for any reason, been made redundant might expect some considerable redundancy pay *and* the slight hope of taking another job, the Tanzanian sisal farmer would probably find no alternative work – nor would he be able to draw social security benefits.

The problem of the redundant Tanzanian sisal worker indicates another area of distress in many parts of the Third World – *unemployment*. According to the Director General of the International Labour Organisation (one of the UN agencies), there were 75 million unemployed people in the Third World in 1971, but this figure was expected to be nearer 300 million in 1980. In most of the 'low income' countries (with a per capita income of £150 (p.a. or less), less than 20% of the labour force is assured of regular wage employment (although many will of course work in subsistence farming, helping to provide enough food for their families). The high unemployment figures can be repeated in most areas of the Third World – the *recorded* unemployment rate for Taiwan was 11.5%, in Puerto Rico 10.4% and in Trinidad 14% (1965). So the difficulties compound – as the infant mortality rate drops due to better medical facilities, more mouths have to be fed from the inadequate food resources available, and these young mouths become hands for which no work is available.

Our list of Third World characteristics could go on. *Adult illiteracy* is generally high, in some cases as high as 90%. Although an illiterate man is able to work in a factory or till a plot of land, he cannot be asked to do a job where he is expected to read instructions. *Tropical and dietary deficiency diseases* sap the strength of many. Bilharzia, a disease contracted through contact with worm-infested water, is particularly debilitating, and although neither malaria nor bilharzia is usually fatal, they cause sufferers to be constantly tired and often run a high temperature. There is a general shortage of medical help to eradicate these diseases. Whereas in the United Kingdom there is one doctor to every 760 people, there is only one doctor to 80,000 in Ethiopia, or one to 35,000 in Nepal.

Perhaps the hazard common to many Third World countries, and one about which we are most frequently made aware, is that of natural calamities. When we are asked to give money for the work of Christian Aid we *expect* to be collecting for a famine/flood/hurricane/earthquake/any other natural disaster in some part or other of the Third World. Indeed, this is the image Christian Aid and Oxfam are desperately anxious to shed, because they are seen by the public merely as relief agencies, rather than as organisations anxious to help Third World countries help themselves.

But having made that point, it is still true that the incidence of natural disasters is much higher in many Third World countries than in the West. We in Britain were made aware of the inconveniences caused by drought in the summers of 1975–6, but had all the advantages of modern technology to help alleviate the situation. The trouble is that the Third World countries do not have the technical know-how nor the financial resources to draw upon in times of natural crises, and so have to rely largely upon the charity of international agencies.

I made the point earlier in the chapter that generalisations about the Third World are dangerous. I am already conscious that I may have allowed this chapter to read like yet another catalogue of disasters and to give the impression that the list of problems I have indicated is common to *all* Third World countries – an impression perhaps given in the otherwise excellent, if somewhat disturbing book by Ronald Sider: *Rich Christians in an Age of Hunger*. Within the Third World there are *enormous contrasts*; contrasts between rich and poor (and no doubt some of us have come across wealthy overseas students who both live luxuriously in this country *and* enjoy frequent holidays on the Continent). Contrasts in size (Brazil has an area of 3,287,000 sq. miles while Gambia has an area of only 4,003 sq. miles); contrasts between town and country; contrasts in climate and physical conditions; contrasts in cultural traditions and in attitudes towards the West, and so on. One can make startling contrasts between one Third World country and another, using the examples above, or one can make equally compelling contrasts within one country. Nigeria has an area of 357,000 sq. miles and a population of 80 million, comprising 250 different tribal groups, and consists of 19 federal states, each with a large measure of autonomy. But the contrast between the federal capital, Lagos, and a small village in North Nigeria is almost unbelievable. It is almost impossible to get across Lagos in the daytime because of the never-moving traffic jams of large company cars, with the result that wealthy Nigerian business men arrive home late to watch their coloured TV sets in their air-conditioned bungalows or enjoy sundowners in palatial lounges. Yet Lagos itself contains some very downtown areas, where Nigerian unemployed young people, by no means all without education, who have moved to the big city in a vain attempt to get work, now live in wretched conditions. Travel 600 miles to a small village near

Kano and you will find compounds made of mud and cowdung, with neither running water nor electricity. The Muslim family living in each compound are polygamous, but with all the wives knowing exactly what is expected of them and whose turn it is to fetch the water or to clean the house. Whereas the family in Lagos would communicate in English, many women in North Nigeria would feel far less competent in using English, and would communicate in Hausa. The only signs of Western sophistication might be a transistor radio and some tins of sardines. But again you might find that one member of that same Hausa family was at secondary school in Kano studying for 'A' levels in Physics and Biology! This enormous contrast between the sophisticated city of Lagos (or Ibadan) and the rest of the country, still very firmly based on agricultural production, much of which is subsistence, is a factor common to Third World countries.

One final generalisation is appropriate before proceeding to consider in more detail some of the economic and environmental problems listed above. Readers might well be in touch with overseas students from Third World countries, and it is to be hoped that some will have offered hospitality to students for a weekend (see Chapter 5). But these students are hardly representative of their countrymen, and often have little contact with, and sometimes appear to have little concern for, their less fortunate fellows. This is to be regretted; but we have to recognise this fact. Indeed we might well find that they are able to live comfortably, travel in Europe more than we can afford to do, and are very sensitive to any suggestion that their home countries are suffering from any of the difficulties we have mentioned. I well remember an occasion when I had invited two Nigerian students to a function when the speaker was a returned VSO. He spoke thoughtfully about his experiences in Nigeria, and concluded by indicating one or two of the problems he had met while working as a volunteer, and instanced the debilitating humidity, and the corruption that he had found in the educational system. The Nigerian instantly jumped to his feet and replied, eloquently defending his country and inviting the speaker to be his guest in Lagos, where he would find everything exactly to his liking!

Although this incident was perfectly innocuous, I do sometimes feel embarrassed for my overseas friends as I listen to 'Third World' missionaries recounting their experiences and am glad that they are not there to listen! This matter of the 'mission image' we in the churches still hold of the Third World, perhaps reinforced by the missionary speakers we have heard recently will be considered in more detail in Chapter 3. But it is sufficient to emphasise here that we need to be aware of the sensitiveness that is felt by many overseas students in the country concerning *our* images of *them* and their countries.

INDEPENDENCE AND AFTER

Independence has come to nearly all the Third World countries in Africa, Asia and the Caribbean within the last generation. Readers' opinions will differ as to the degree of development and benevolent rule or, on the other hand, of oppression and cultural destruction that the colonial period brought about, and it is no part of this book to take a stance one way or the other. More to the point is the views of the countries themselves towards their colonial past. Political leaders like Nkrumah, Nyerere, Gandhi and Manley saw their countries' position as colonies in terms of subjugation. The Swahili word 'uhuru' means 'freedom from slavery', and this was the slogan of Nyerere's political party (TANU) that fought for, and won, the fight for Independence. On one occasion the first federal Prime Minister of Nigeria, Azikwe, made a statement in which he declared that his country 'was groaning' under an unnjust system. He could have been referring to the appalling lack of medical facilities or schools, or poor communications in Nigeria. But he wasn't; he was referring to the subjugation of his country by a colonial power.

Many Third World countries, therefore, felt a sense of grievance at their colonial status, and regard political independence as a prize they have fought for and won, sometimes at great cost. Indeed, this might be true for countries like Zaïre, which does have a legacy of Belgian exploitation to live down, although there is less evidence of direct oppression by the British colonial masters. British exploitation took more subtle forms! It would be fair to indicate that in general Britain willingly accceded to the requests for Independence, however, provided that certain constitutional requirements were met, and with the Independence of India on August 30, 1947, the long train of Independence celebrations began. In fact 44 countries have become politically independent from Britain since then, all except two remaining loosely associated with Great Britain in the new Commonwealth relationship. (There are 46 countries in the Commonwealth, including Great Britain – January 1982.) But more problems began than were solved when the Union Jack was lowered and replaced by the new national flag. Countries had to prove themselves, first to their own people, and then to the world. Deportations should perhaps be seen as one of the minor teething troubles of a new country, as political leaders flexed their muscles and showed their former colonial masters who now held the power.

It would be an over-simplification to suggest that these new nations have to choose only between capitalism or communism as the best political philosophy for them to follow, because a number of them have – quite rightly – evolved a political framework of their own. But in *broad general* terms, countries can choose to follow *either* a system based upon private enterprise, like Kenya or Liberia, *or* one based upon a socialist philosophy, like Tanzania, *or* accept a period of strong military control like Ethiopia. The latter model is often the result of the overthrow of a corrupt capitalist government, as happened in Ghana. The interest arises when a country resolves to work out its own political philosophy, as has happened in Tanzania, or make clear its own stance vis a vis its ex-colonial master, as has happened in Francophone Africa.

Following independence, Third World countries have had to decide about their new political alignments. Were they to remain loyal to Britain (or France, or Belgium, or Portugal) or choose their own political allies? Undoubtedly Britain has recently realised the diplomatic value of maintaining firm allies in the Third World, particularly as Russia, China, Cuba and the United States of America have also seen their interests furthered by courting certain Third World countries, and in some cases offering financial aid. This aid, whether given in the form of grants, loans or skilled manpower, is sometimes interpreted by the receiving countries as a not very subtle form of buying back loyalty. Although this motive may not in fact be foremost in the thinking of the donor country, nevertheless the suspicion must be taken into account when evaluating the different perceptions of the aid process.

Another area of sensitivity concerns Britain's attitude towards the white minorities in Southern Africa. Certainly the political and constitutional background influences leading up to the recent confusion and waste of life and resources in Zimbabwe are very complex, and makes it difficult for Christians to know what stance to take. This dilemma of choice is not a problem for the rest of independent Africa, however. They point out that although

Britain insisted on majority rule before giving her other colonies independence, she was not willing to take a firm stand in Zimbabwe, which was indeed a colony, having in fact *chosen* colonial status to Britain instead of amalgamation with South Africa in 1923. Therefore Britain ought not to have allowed UDI in the first place, much less allow it to continue for over fifteen years. Similarly Britain's attitude towards apartheid in South Africa is seen by many as ambivalent. They argue that while outwardly maintaining a position of moral rectitude, many commercial concerns continue to uphold the white-dominated regime by trading with South Africa. They see the regime as totally evil, and regard it as their task to overthrow it – hence the ongoing guerilla warfare in the front-line states in Southern Africa.

This deep conviction of the wrongness of the existing apartheid regime in South Africa has expressed itself in a number of ways. However we may feel about these, Western observers should take account of this revulsion towards apartheid when international incidents occur. Thus there was disagreement in 1976 concerning Commonwealth member countries taking part in international sports competitions with South Africa, and the subsequent withdrawal by a number of Third World members from the Commonwealth games. Again, the 1981-82 Test tour of India was nearly cancelled because one member of the team had some previous professional involvement in South Africa. One can expect this kind of extreme sensitiveness of continue until the South African dilemma has been resolved.

Another area of post-independence sensitivity concerns expatriate personnel working or living in Third World countries. Governments have been anxious to tear down the last bastions of colonialism like segregated clubs and organisations, and all such groups have to be open to members of all nationalities. Technical personnel now working in these countries are regarded as the servants of the new independent government, and thus Europeans are treated with less respect and deference than formerly. This desire *to be seen to be in control* also extends to mission strategy and deployment. As a general rule, societies have been the slowest to hand over the controls to the local church, and have been particularly reluctant to allow them to control the postings and movements of expatriate missionary staff. Although I cannot trace the source of the ensuing comment, I have every reason to believe it is reliable! When finally the missionary societies did hand over control in one Central African country, one of the first activities of the local church authority was to organise a 'general post' of all missionaries – just to show who was now the boss! (The complex issue of ongoing missionary activity in the Third World is considered in more detail in Chapter 3, but the point about Third World sensitivity to expatriates working in newly-independent countries needs to be thoroughly appreciated.

'Newness' on the international scene, therefore, is one phenomenon common to most Third World countries in Africa, India, the Far East and the Caribbean. Growing into meaningful nationhood is likely to produce a whole series of problems and adjustments which we would do well to try to understand. Two further internal areas of friction need to be mentioned. 'Nationhood' is indeed the course plotted as the road ahead by the political leaders, but it may not be easy for some countries where there are a number of ethnic and/or religious differences that cause deep division. We have already noticed the size and complexity of Nigeria. These differences in tribe, language and religion caused the deep divisions and rivalries that finally led to the tragic civil war in that country in 1966. The Ibo people in the East felt that their interests would be best served by breaking away from the main political unit of Nigeria and going it alone as the new country of Biafra. This secession was challenged by General Gowan and the country stayed together, but only after a bloody and wasteful civil war which has left a legacy of suspicion between the federating parts of Nigeria. Pakistan, divided by 3,000 miles of North India, was so impossible a political unit to keep together that the country finally split into Pakistan and Bangladesh. Although those two countries have suffered more than most through either tribal and ethnic rivalry or through the sheer impossibility of their geographical situation, lack of real ethnic or political unity is an ongoing hazard in the Third World.

Political instability is the other hazard of which we are only too well aware. This is often triggered off by the overthrow of a corrupt government and the consequent emergence of a strong military regime and a period of severe military rule. There have been no fewer than 150 wars within the Third World since 1945, 50 of which have been fought on African soil, and no less than half the countries within Africa have been troubled by at least one period of war. 75% of these wars have been civil wars, aimed either at overthrowing the existing regime or fought between tribal or religious groups within a single nation state.

All this can mean only a fearful waste of money on buying military hardware. Although most countries in independent Africa need all the financial resources they can lay hands on to aid their national educational and medical development plans, military expenditure in Africa is increasing faster than anywhere else in the World except the Middle East.

One reason for this ongoing instability is the sheer lack of trained personnel ready to take over the responsibilities of government; although there was a cadre of graduates and others able to assume positions of political leadership in some countries like India and Ghana, there certainly was not in Botswana or Zambia, where graduates could be counted on the fingers of four hands! As James Kirkman suggests in his critique of British Colonial policy in the fifties and sixties:

> The steps taken by the British Government to prepare these countries for independence, though not ideal, were adequate. If you teach a child to swim the breast-stroke, he will not necessarily become an Olympic champion, or even get along very fast in the water, but if, having taught him, you throw him in at the deep end of the pool, you do so on the reasonable assumption that he will be able to keep afloat. Unfortunately in the case of some other territories, the swimming lessons have not even produced competence at the breast-stroke, and sometimes, it is as if they have been thrown into the pool with a couple of bricks round their necks.[1]

SOME OF THE PROBLEMS FACING THE THIRD WORLD

Poverty and the Third World

Possibly Third World countries would more easily overcome the hazards connected with 'newness' if they were not also bedevilled with all the other difficulties listed earlier in this chapter.

One of the most pressing – and the most difficult to overcome – is the overall problem of poverty. Perhaps this is one of the concepts that we have come to associate most completely with the Third World; when somebody mentions India or Africa we think of potbellied children, droughts and a general picture of poverty. Possibly we are being fed these kinds of images by some of the agencies involved in relief programmes in the Third World. A recent 'Sunday' programme included a dialogue between a number of these organisations, and one or two representatives openly admitted that to present such harrowing pictures of the Third World persuaded the public to give more generously than they would otherwise have done. This is unfortunate, because in the long run such action can do only a disservice to the countries concerned.

As we have already seen, national standards of living are generally measured by two indices – GNP and Per Capita Income. Statistics hide enormous diversities in living standards; the GNP (per capita) of India, for example, is £75 and indeed India *is* a very poor country, with a very real problem of ongoing starvation in some areas. But we should also appreciate that large Indian cities have their millionaires and their prosperous middle class. The per capita income figure (income per head of population) cannot bring out the extremes of wealth in a given country – a few people are extremely wealthy, while the majority remain poor. For example in Mexico in the two decades 1950-69, the per capita income increased by 3% in real terms, but the richest 10% of the population pushed up *their share* of the total national income from 49% to 51% – more than half of the total wealth of the country was monopolised by 10% of the people! On the other hand the share of the national income for the poorest 40% of the population actually decreased from 14%-11%. Again, in Peru, the top 0.1% of the working population enjoy 19.9% of the national income – in other words, nearly 1/5 of the total wealth of that country is locked up in the bank accounts or wealthy houses of one in every thousand members of the population![2] One study has indicated that inequalities in income are generally greater in the poor countries than in the rich. In the developed countries, the upper 10% of the income earners receive about 30% of the total pre-tax income, whereas the comparative figure for the Third World countries would be about 40%.[3]

Before we attempt to reach our conclusions about poverty, we should bear in mind two relevant factors. Two items that figure prominently in every British family's budget are transport and fuel costs. As fares and oil prices rise, so the commuters see a greater percentage of their income being swallowed up by the cost of travel to and from work, and they come home to pay higher bills for their electricity and oil. Neither of these items is nearly as significant in most Third World countries – only in the large cities is there any evidence of commuting!

But having made these adjustments in our thinking, we still have to come back to the inescapable conclusion that many people living in the Third World *are* living in a state of poverty. Whatever statistics we use – per capita income, infant mortality and life expectancy, nutritional deficiency, the high incidence of debilitating diseases – all force us to the conclusion that the lives of many people and indeed many Christians in the Third World are conditioned by poverty, and ill health and that they have little chance of improving their lot. Their poverty is both *relative*, as the graph shows, and it is also *absolute*. Although our modern technological society has brought 'us' and 'them' much nearer and, perhaps more significantly, has given them a vision of the benefits and comforts development can offer, the two remain worlds apart.

Table 3
The Widening Gap

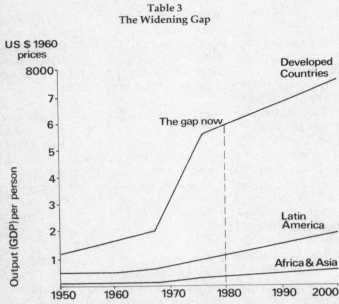

Taken from: Worlds Apart and World Development Report 1976

The Brandt Report: *North – South – a Programme for Survival* has served to bring the poverty of parts of the Third World into sharper relief. This report indicates that 29 nations of the world can be found in two poverty belts. One stretches across the middle of Africa from the Sahara to Lake Nyasa, and the other from the two Yemens and Afghanistan across South Asia. In

these poverty belts live 13% of the population of the Third World
– about 258 million – and the *overall* per capita income is less than
£75 per annum. Bear in mind that within them may be found
some very sophisticated cities like Lagos, Nairobi and Delhi,
and one is again reminded of the enormous difficulties involved
in achieving an exact system of classification – and also of the fact
that a lot of people in the Third World are today very poor
indeed.

Two further indices of poverty need to be considered here. The
first contains the sort of food many people eat for their stable
diet. Nutrition experts regard a dietary intake of approximately
2,500 calories a day, including an adequate protein content (fish,
eggs, meat, milk etc.), as a basic requirement for proper health.
Too much carbohydrate (rice, potatoes) makes for fatness without
proper bodily growth.

Table 4
Daily Calorie and Protein Consumption

Country	Daily calorie intake per capita	Daily total protein level (grams per day)
India	1,810	45.4
Philippines	2,000	50.5
Nigeria	2,180	59.5
Colombia	2,200	48.9
Peru	2,340	54.1
UK	3,150	87.5
USA	3,200	95.6

Table 4 indicates the position of many Third World countries
with regard to diet *deficiency*. An unbalanced diet lowers resis-
tance to debilitating diseases like kwashiorkor and malaria and
also impairs the structural development of the human brain,
which reaches 90% of its normal structural development in the
first four years of a child's life. This malnutrition produces
millions of retarded children. The following extract is a poignant
illustration of this tragic situation.

Little Marli, a happy six-year-old girl from Rio de Janeiro is just one of
these. Little Marli looked normal in every way. Healthy. Happy.
There was just one thing wrong with her. She couldn't learn. At first
teachers thought perhaps her difficulty was psychological, the result
of neglect in a family of eleven children. Her younger sister had the
same problem. But after careful observation and testing, it was evident
that Marli, a child of Brazil's poor and wretched favelas (slums), was

unable to learn because as an infant her malnourished body could not produce a healthy brain.[4]

Some children do not even survive to the age of 6! The infant mortality rate for many Third World countries is much higher than for the West. If we translate Table 5 into more realistic terms, 49 children out of every 50 born in the United Kingdom survive till their first birthday, but 6 Indian babies out of 50 and 8 Tanzanian babies never see their first birthday.

Table 5
Infant Mortality (No. of deaths between birth and one year per 1,000 live births)

Nigeria	163
Tanzania	150
Malawi	142
India	122
Pakistan	113
Ghana	63
UK	16
Sweden	8

The Population Explosion

It may at first sight seem strange to follow on these remarks with a discussion of the population explosion in the Third World, but we should remember that there is a close relationship between affluence and a decline in population. There are obvious reasons for this. As families in the West enjoy a higher standard of living with all the trappings that go along with it (larger and more comfortable houses, better education for their children, overseas holidays etc.) – and a more scientific understanding of birth control, so they resolve to limit their families to a size that can gain the maximum advantage from these luxuries.

A personal illustration may make this point more graphically. I decided to 'treat' my family to a winter holiday on the Costa Brava recently, and we all enjoyed the winter sunshine enormously. Whereas I found I could just afford to take my wife and two small daughters with me, it would have been out of the question to have taken seven or eight children! Of course, this problem would never arise for most families in India or Tanzania as they cannot afford to take an annual holiday in any case.

The population explosion, or the average population growth

per annum, in the developing countries is 2.4%[5] compared with the United Kingdom 0.1%, and this means that some countries may well double their population in one generation. The population growth in Latin America is 2.7% per annum, and on this calculation the population of this area in 2000 AD would be in the region of 2,000,000,000 – or just about the size of the total world population in 1975. Other statistics are equally frightening – the population of West Africa would be 200,000,000, of India 958,000,000, and of Brazil 205,000,000. The population of countries like Nigeria will double in one generation.

Table 6
Population Growth in Selected Third World Countries, mid 1978 – mid 1979

Country	mid 1978 (000)	mid 1979	Growth Rate (%)
Ethiopia	30,982	31,799	+2.5
Bangladesh	84,655	86,961	+2.8
Brazil	119,461	122,879	+2.9
Columbia	25,573	26,122	+2.3
Nepal	13,625	13,947	+2.3
Nigeria	80,563	82,503	+2.5
Zaïre	26,770	27,535	+2.7

N.B. All the countries (103) with a population increase of more than 2% per annum are in the Third World.

(Source: World Bank Report, 1980).

The overriding reason for this population explosion is not a marked rise in fertility, but a spectacular fall in the death rate. One economist has referred to the present population bulge in the Third World as 'the DDT generation'. As prophylactics have been introduced from the West, the fatalities from malaria have dropped spectacularly, and preventive treatments have reduced the incidence of such diseases as yellow fever, smallpox, typhoid and cholera enormously. In just three years from 1945-48 Sri Lanka reduced its death rate by the same percentage that it took West Europe 300 years to accomplish, due largely to the successful control of malaria. When I first visited the coast in Ghana, I stumbled across an overgrown cemetery and was just able to decipher the details on many of the graves. Most were graves of young men who had come to the 'white man's grave' one hundred and fifty years ago and contracted malaria or some tropical disease within weeks of their arrival, and in the absence of prophylactic medicine, had died. But I then proceeded to enjoy four very healthy years in Ghana!

Thousands of expatriates go to Third World countries today to work, and enjoy perhaps a better standard of health than they would in foggy Britain. Although this would not be quite true of the native population, it is still true that they do enjoy a much longer expectancy of life than they would have done fifty years ago. It is indeed ironic that the transfer of *medical* knowledge has been perhaps the most successful of all areas of skills transferred from the West to the Third World, and one that has added to their problems. It has produced an increasing 'burden of dependency' – a high proportion of young people who demand to be educated but are not assisting the overall development of the economy. In most developing countries, 40% of the population is under the age of 20 (compared with 20% in Europe). This burden is cumulative: as the bulge moves up so they in turn become parents and the majority of young people gets still greater and the problem worsens.

Two other points need to be made in this context. The first is concerned with the relationship between this population explosion and overall economic growth. Whereas the preventative medical strategies used to reduce infant mortality can be put into operation without any co-operation from the villagers themselves – all that needs to be done to reduce the incidence of malaria in a village is to spray every house, or to reduce child mortality through measles is to line up the children and give them an injection, for example – these actions won't produce an agrarian revolution! To teach the farmers to rotate their crops or to change the crops they grow in order to maximise their cash return requires much more co-operation from the people themselves. So it would not be true to suggest that a growing population is a 'plus' for the Third World at this point in time – more mouths to feed represent a major obstacle to continued development.

The other point concerns birth control. Family planning is clearly an essential ingredient in all Third World countries' demographic planning, but three basic requirements are needed if any programme is to succeed. The first is the availability of cheap contraceptive techniques. By and large this requirement has been met, and the inter-uterine coil seems to be proving both effective and cheap, and has only minimal unfortunate side-effects, provided it is properly fitted by a qualified medical auxiliary. It is doubly important in a primitive rural society that the contraceptive device used *is* effective, because the occasional and unforseen failures will damage confidence for the future. Secondly, there has to be an effective machinery to carry out the programme – available personnel with the necessary medical training, but above all sympathy and diplomacy, so that they can relate to, and help to dispel the prejudices of, the people living in the rural areas with whom they will be working. Most important, the people themselves need to accept birth control as both necessary and culturally acceptable. For many Third World societies a large family has for centuries become an accepted tradition, and a man's esteem is to some extent measured by the number of children he has managed to rear. The Psalmist extols the man who has his quiver full of arrows (Psalm 127:3–5)! In a subsistence society, the more children that grow into adolescence, the more they can help on the family farm, and later they may bring in marriage dowries. Most important, a large family is a guarantee of security in old age. Unlike our nuclear family, where we tend to frown upon grandparents living with the younger generation, it is customary for the extended family to live together, and it is unusual for old people to live by themselves, particularly in the rural areas. So the more children that are around, the better the chance that the parents will be properly cared for in their old age. In other words, children are regarded as a form of social insurance. Thus the peasant who persists in producing large numbers of children may be acting quite rationally from his point of view, as well as fulfilling the norms of the society to which he belongs. It is no good telling him that large families are contrary to the community interest – he just won't believe you!

As part of a recent campaign to encourage peasants in India to accept birth control methods, a poster was produced showing two families. One family were clearly well dressed and content, and the other clearly were equally poor – badly dressed and looking bedraggled. The first family had two children, the second seven. The poster created a considerable impact upon the many who looked at it. But their reaction was summed up in the thoughtful comment of one family; 'What a shame that the more prosperous couple had only two children to help share their happiness.'!

Indeed, birth control is becoming accepted in many Third World countries, but this acceptance is a slow process and most face an immediate problem of too many mouths to feed, with the added difficulty that many of those mouths do not belong to productive hands, but rather belong to minds that demand education – a long term investment with no immediate return.

Unemployment in the Third World

Too many mouths to feed – and too many hands to employ! As we have already seen, nearly all Third World countries suffer from the demoralizing problem of increasing unemployment. The Indian case will illustrate this issue clearly. In 1961, official unemployment amounted to 9 millions, and the employment objective of the 5 year plan was to create 14 million new jobs. But it was estimated that during theperiod 1961-66 17 million new workers would be joining the labour market, and thus the last state was worse than the first.

The figures quoted here and on page 23 are only *official* estimates of unemployment, and as such are totally unreliable. Indeed, there is no single reliable method of calculating them, because very few Third World countries have any unemployment exchanges or social security systems. So we can be reasonably sure that the real figures are higher than those quoted. Moreover, many more are *under-employed*, comprising groups in society who are doing jobs not compatible with their education, like young people with school certificate working as cooks or garden boys; and, more significantly, many whose total employment consists of helping a member of their family on their farm. It may well include an army of shoe cleaners, match and cigarette sellers, car cleaners and the like who add very little to the total volume of a country's economic output.

Unemployment in the Third World is especially chronic in the larger and usually new towns. There are a number of reasons for this. Part of the contemporary social revolution in many Third World countries is the drift from the villages to the towns, partly to escape from a primitive rural society and partly in an attempt to earn money in order to buy the trappings of modernity. But, for a number of reasons, the jobs aren't available, and the young people who have come looking for work join the evergrowing army of unemployed who inevitably turn to petty crime and live in appalling conditions. Add to these the growing number of *graduates* – lawyers and arts graduates whose skills cannot be fully used at this stage in the country's development – and one has ready material for urban crime and political instability. Again this is a tragic situation when so much of this wasted skill ought to be harnessed to assist the country's overall development.

The Economic Base of the Third World

One final economic hazard that demands further consideration concerns the narrow agricultural base on which the economy of many Third World countries rests. As we have already seen (page 22) most depend for their export earnings on one or two primary products, which are subject to very considerable price fluctuations on the world market. In 1978, 57% of the export earnings of the Third World countries (81% if oil is included) came from selling primary commodities in their raw, or nearly raw state. *The economic survival* of some of these countries depends upon a single commodity. Zambia depends upon copper for 94% of its export earnings; Mauritius earns 90% of its earnings from sugar, and the Gambia, 85% from groundnuts and groundnut oil. The bulk of the processing and marketing of these commodities is carried out in the West, with the result that the returns to the developing country producers tend to be less than 25% of the final consumer prices. Indeed the trading relationship between rich *industrial* countries and poor *primary* producers is a very unequal, and some would suggest, an unfair one. Whereas the West can rely on a wide diversity of manufactured goods – Britain's exports range from shirts to steel, from grand pianos to matches – many Third World countries are confined to agricultural or mineral products that in some cases they were forced to produce 100 years ago. At times British industrialists forced Third World competitors out of a market that might have proved competitive to their monopoly. Whereas for example in the 17th and 18th centuries Indian textiles and spices were in great demand in the West because of the *technological superiority* of Indian producers, the cotton magnates of North-West England saw these imports as a threat to their new-found source of wealth, and (through their representatives in Parliament) imposed a 75% duty on Indian textiles. Within the period 1814–44, Indian cotton exports shrank from 1,250,000 pieces to 63,000 – a drop of 95%. (Strenuous efforts were also made to prevent the emergence of an industrial sector in the American colonies, but they preferred to fight for, and win, their independence from Britain rather than accept such devastating constraints upon their economy.)

But British fiscal policy changed drastically in the middle of the 19th century. The manufacturing interests, now secure in their sources of acquiring wealth, argued that they would do better by adopting a policy of free trade, which in effect developed into a specialization of trade between themselves and the colonies.

British manufacturers sold the products of Victorian supremacy – a wide range of industrial goods, as well as their finance and expertise (in the form of personnel) to their newly acquired colonies, and in return bought from them the agricultural products that they needed to satisfy their more sophisticated tastes, or the raw materials they needed in order to manufacture the goods they then exported round the world.

It would be difficult to draw up an economic balance sheet for imperialism. There is no doubt that the imperial powers opened up the colonies to outside ideas and influences; they certainly provided both an *economic* infrastructure (roads, railways etc.) and an *administrative* machinery (a system of Government, offices and judicial system) that have made subsequent development possible. They provided schools and hospitals which have undoubtedly made the lives of millions more pleasant. But the charge of economic exploitation is one from which they cannot escape. Either the prices paid for the agricultural goods – cocoa, tea, sisal, cotton etc. – were far too low, with the result that the peasants working on the European-owned farms were paid only an absolutely minimal wage, or countries found themselves compelled to concentrate on growing only one crop, and thus laid themselves wide open to the vagaries of climatic hazards, changing world demand, or the final risk of alternative crops supplanting the demand for the one crop they have developed.

Hans Singer, United Nations economist, wrote:

> It is a matter of historical fact that ever since the 1870's the trend of prices has been heavily against sellers of food and raw materials and in favour of the sellers of manufactured articles. The statistics are open to doubt and to objection in detail, but the general story which they tell us is unmistakable.[6]

Thus the Government of Tanzania found that one tractor cost 5 tons of sisal in 1963. In 1970 the same tractor cost 10 tons of sisal. In the late '70s sisal has been virtually replaced by nylon and corrugated paper. It is a very unusual sight nowadays to see a new sack used on a British farm – everything is bagged in corrugated paper. Advantaged: the British farmers; the losers – the Tanzanian sisal growers and labourers.

This theme of economic exploitation has been dealt with more fully in Walter Rodney's book: *How Europe Underdeveloped Africa* (Bogle L'Ouverture Publications 1972). This is described by one sociologist as the story of the 'frightful history of the rape, retardation and deliberate destruction of the peoples and economies of the African continent for the benefit of the people of Europe'. It is clearly a very critical book, but Christians should not imagine that they are excused from reading this book because Rodney held very extreme left wing political views. They should read Morris Stuart's: *The Black Mirror – a Reflection*, published by the Race Relations Unit of the BCC at 50p. This booklet, also written by a West Indian, is a summary of a series of articles in *Crusade*, and spells out a black Christian's response to Christian Europe's exploitation of Africa. Although perhaps not a very cosy book for the British Christian, it is nevertheless a book that he should make a point of reading.

Although there is little value in castigating ourselves for the sins of our fathers, there is a Christian dimension to be considered in this whole matter of colonial exploitation. It is a consistent scriptural teaching that God lifts up the poor and disadvantaged and casts down the wealthy and powerful, if their wealth has been acquired by oppressing the poor or if they fail to share their wealth and feed the hungry. (See Amos 4:1; 5: 10–18; 2:6). As Christians we cannot stand by while others starve, and we certainly cannot allow ourselves to get rich through exploiting others.

Some of these economic hazards are the result of men's rapacity, and could be averted if we were more willing to share the world's resources on a more equitable basis. Having made that statement, however, the writer is the first to realise that this change of heart is an exceedingly difficult one to initiate, and would cause tremendous repercussions on the entire world market scene. It is easy to suggest that the Western companies pay much more for the primary products they buy from the Third World, but I wonder how many of us complained bitterly when coffee and chocolate prices last rocketed!

The Environmental Problems of the Third World

On the other hand, some of the *environmental* problems that bedevil certain Third World countries seem to be almost beyond the control of man – are they in the hands of God? I wish I knew the answer to that problem! Some Third World countries are particularly exposed to natural disasters like the disastrous earthquakes of 1970 in Peru and 1972 in Nicaragua, or the hurricanes that occur regularly in the Caribbean, or the droughts that caused such enormous loss of both animal and human life in the

Sahel in 1975–76 – or, on the other hand, the floods in parts of India and Pakistan in the last three or four years. It is quite true to point out that such hazards do not occur exclusively in the Third World, but their incidence is greater – and, much more important, these countries do not have the resources to enable them either to rehabilitate or to take action to avoid the worst excesses of some of these calamities. There were floods along the coast of Kent and Norfolk in the winter of 1977, and several million pounds of damage was done, but the Government immediately arranged a programme of relief and agreed that much of the cost of the flood damage should properly be met from Government funds. In addition, individuals whose property was damaged were able to claim compensation if their belongings had been properly insured. Similarly, when earthquakes occur in Japan, government help is immediately provided, and in fact new techniques are being developed whereby the foundations of houses in an earthquake zone are specially reinforced. But there are not the material or financial resources available in many Third World countries to help those whose homes have been destroyed in an earthquake or whose cattle have died in the drought. There were no enormous reservoirs built in the Sahel from which the peasants could water their cattles; so they died, and so did many peasants.

Organisations like *Tear Fund* and *War on Want* do send help to disaster areas when these natural calamities occur, but it is much more difficult for a community to rehabilitate itself after the earthquake if there are not sufficient resources available, and this is the situation that many Third World countries have to accept.

Medical and Educational Facilities

Some environmental problems are being met and to some extent overcome by human instrumentality. It is possible to avert plagues of locusts by massive spraying programmes. Similarly children can be immunised against epidemic diseases like whooping cough, measles etc. But such prophylactic treatment demands adequate medical facilities, and once again these are sadly lacking in many Third World countries, as table 7 shows. In fact this table offers a very incomplete picture, because we know little about medical facilities that are available in the hospitals, or the supplies that get through. In Zaïre, for example, a missionary doctor friend reported that on one occasion 150,000 tablets out of 200,000 aspirins disappeared from a bonded warehouse! This is the more serious when one realises that aspirins cost £10 for 1,000 in Zaïre, as opposed to 62p in England (in 1977). The general pattern seems to be that only about 50% of the medical supplies get through to the hospitals or dispensaries in Zaïre. As I wrote this paragraph, I had one eye on the TV news report that a team of English surgeons had completed another heart transplant, and the technique of surgical replacements is one that is being used more frequently in our hospitals. Very often hospitals in the Third World struggle to maintain the equipment to carry out the simplest of operations, due, not just to the lack of surgical expertise, but rather to the lack of capital available to purchase and service sophisticated equipment.

Table 7
Medical Facilities in the Third World
Number of people per physician available

Ethiopia	69,340
Bangladesh	9,350
Nepal	36,450
Zaïre	27,950
Tanzania	20,800
Nigeria	25,400
UK	750
Switzerland	590

N.B. This table gives no indication of the distribution of medical facilities; people in the towns have a much better chance of seeing a doctor than those in the rural areas.

Perhaps a word of warning should be sounded here. It would be quite wrong to convey the impression that medical facilities throughout the Third World are appalling, and that any expatriate who goes to India or Africa risks life and limb by so doing. This is just not so; most of the important towns do support large hospitals, many of which are well provided for with up-to-date equipment. It is the men and women in the bush who suffer. Often they find themselves a long way from the nearest hospital, and cannot see a doctor when they need one. But some countries are tackling this problem in a realistic way. Tanzania, for example, has recently set up a very sensible scheme of training medical auxiliaries who receive enough training to enable them to diagnose and treat the most common diseases like bilharzia and malaria, but to recognise their limitations and refer more difficult cases to the next rung in the medical ladder. Although perhaps

we might find the very simple and direct medical examination a
little 'thin' (the auxilary identifies some obvious symptoms,
looks down his chart if he hasn't managed to memorise the
appropriate diagnosis by heart, and prescribes some pills); at
least this system does offer a very considerable measure of relief
to many who would otherwise spend a lifetime of discomfort.
(Readers who are interested to know more of this experiment are
recommended to see the video tape *A Fair Share of What Little We
Have*, made as a *Horizon* programme by BBC in August 1977).

We in the West have come to regard universal education as a
basic human right. And indeed this is the aim of UNESCO – to
make available to all children everywhere a measure of education
that will enable them to take a full and active part in adult life. But
once again this ideal is dependent upon the availability of
sufficient teachers and schools to make the ideal a reality.

Table 8
Education in the Third World

	Primary enrolments as % of age group	Secondary enrolments as % of age group	Adult Literacy Rate*
Ethiopia	23	6	7*
Bangladesh	73	25	23
Nepal	27	18	19
Tanzania	57	3	63
Nigeria	49	39	
UK	100	76	98
Switzerland	92	69	99

* The *overall* literacy rate of the poorest countries in the Third World increased
from 10% to 23% in the period 1960-1975.

NEW SOLUTIONS FOR NEW COUNTRIES

So – where do we go from here? I set out determined not to write
yet another chronicle of the woes that beset the Third World,
because this can so easily become counter-productive. It is a tale
that has been told too often, and after a while we find we can take
no more, and in psychological self-defence, switch off. Yet I am
bound to tell the story as it is, and it would be dishonest to ignore
the many problems that have aggravated the Third World for so
long, and will undoubtedly continue to do so for some time to
come. But it would be equally wrong to ignore efforts that are
being made, both from outside and by national governments
themselves, to alleviate those problems and help these countries

develop. Because this point is crucial – they are developing, and although the 5% annual average growth rate achieved in the 'Development Decade' must be considered side-by-side with the continuing population explosion,[5] yet it would still verify President Nyerere's comment that when his country was under the colonial yoke, it was administered, but once it became independent, it developed! And Tanzania has developed, as the following paragraphs indicate.

Tanzania and African Socialism

It will be interesting to take a closer look at the strategies for development that Tanzania has used. The goal of development is common to all Third World countries, but often the methods used to reach that goal will differ. In the years immediately following Independence Tanzania suffered from nearly all the economic and environmental problems that have been mentioned 1above. The years 1965–67 were characterised not only by droughts and the failure of the staple agricultural crops, but also by the complete collapse of the world market in sisal, her biggest single export earner. Her economic problems were exacerbated by political issues: Nyerere's determined moral stand against the West for attempting to interfere in his decision to allow the East German Democratic Republic to set up an Embassy in Dar Es Salaam in 1964, and especially against Britain for allowing Rhodesia to declare UDI in 1965, cost him several million pounds of West European aid. In 1967 Nyerere issued a document that has become almost a classic in development studies – the Arusha Declaration. Starting with a critique of capitalism, the Declaration argues that Tanzania is seeking true (African) socialism, and to that end is involved in a war against poverty and oppression. But hitherto the people have used the wrong weapon – money. 'It is as if we have said "Money is the basis of development. Without money there can be no development."' But, argues Nyerere, money brings with it enormous risks; the money isn't there, or to borrow too much money from other countries will endanger the new nation's independence.

> How can we depend upon foreign governments and companies for the major part of our development without giving to them a great part of our freedom to act as we please? The truth is that we cannot. Therefore the only proper way forward for Tanzania is to pursue a policy of self-reliance.

Industries will come and money will come but their foundation is THE
PEOPLE and their HARD WORK especially in AGRICULTURE. (Sic). This is
the meaning of self-reliance. Our emphasis should therefore be on:
(a) The Land and Agriculture (b) The People (c) The Policy of Self-
Reliance and (d) Good Leadership. *(The Arusha Declaration)*.

The Arusha Declaration goes on to state a case for a policy of
fierce Socialism, forbidding Government leaders to hold shares
in companies, to hold Directorships, to receive two or more
salaries or to rent out houses. Subsequently Nyerere has instituted a policy of 'Ujamaa' or self-help villages, in which all party
members devote part of their time to working on a cooperative
basis. Their time and opportunity to earn any money for themselves is strictly monitored by the members of the party living in
the village. This policy has not been without its teething troubles;
some tribes whose tradition was pastoral have been forced to
change their way of life and join the Ujamaa villages; some
peasants have resented the strict control over their opportunity
to become 'capitalists', and many living in the towns have tended
to scorn the entire exercise.

Yet it has worked, in that it has put Tanzania on the path to
development. The country has survived the difficulties of the late
'60s, and has embarked upon some very thoughtful experiments
in education and public health. Nyerere has argued that Tanzania
needs to work out her own philosophy of education and
development, and must no longer merely follow the path laid
down for her by her former colonial master.

Perhaps it should be added that Nyerere is himself a convinced
Christian and has constantly affirmed that he is not a Marxist,
although he has considerable respect for certain aspects of the
Chinese way of life.

Tanzania provides an interesting illustration of a rather unusual
strategy for development; very much the result of one man's
thoughts and reactions to a local situation, the policy is fiercely
self-reliant and depends upon the whole-hearted cooperation of
the citizens of the country. To some extent this cooperation has
been forthcoming, and considerable progress has been made in
Tanzania since Independence. But it would be foolish to suggest
that the Arusha Declaration should provide a blueprint for every
country in Africa, at least without local modification in each case.

The Green Revolution

Another interesting and to some extent successful experience in India and parts of S. E. Asia has been 'the green revolution'. Based upon the experiments of an American agronomist in Mexico, new strains of wheat and rice, offering very high yields, were produced and introduced in the famine-stricken areas of the Punjab, Haryana and Uttar Pradesh in North India. These high yielding variety (HYV) dwarf seeds quickly led to an increase in these three states of 3.8 million tons of wheat over the pre-drought figure of 10.7 million tons – a dramatic increase of 35% in one year! 'Miracle wheat' and 'miracle rice' as they became known were quickly introduced to Pakistan, Bangladesh, Sri Lanka, Korea, the Philippines and Indonesia, and have increased food production there very considerably, in some cases making double-cropping possible. In Pakistan, for example, wheat production increased by 50% in two years, and in the same period rice production in Sri Lanka increased by 34%.

It would be foolish to deny that 'the green revolution' has had dramatic effects in helping a number of Third World countries towards self-reliance in food production, yet more recently a number of serious criticisms of it have been made.[7] The bumper harvests of HYV wheat and rice are critically dependent on a number of inputs, which must be used in the right proportion at the right time. These are irrigation, drainage, fertilizers and pesticides. These all require capital, and in effect this meant that the advantages of the 'miracle seeds' were restricted to those farmers who were already progressive and relatively prosperous, while the great mass of peasant farmers remain untouched. In effect, one of the side-effects of 'the green revolution', therefore, has been to widen the gap between the poor peasants and the wealthy entrepreneurial farmers. The point was well made in a comment by Mrs Judith Hart;

> Development must not result in prosperous farmers growing richer while peasants grow poorer; those displaced by agricultural development must not become the new urban unemployed; those most in need of food must have the opportunity to buy it.

CONCLUSION

Finally, what of the next ten years for the Third World? To attempt to make any accurate predictions would amount to an act of total folly, and I do not intend to waste readers' time by crystal-ball gazing. There are so many unpredictable factors, but although those unpredictables may well cause end results that we cannot foresee, it will be worth considering some of those external influences that will certainly change the future course of events in the Third World! In the first place, much will depend upon the possible 'discovery' (to use a loaded word in Third World vocabulary!) of valuable mineral deposits. The refining of crude oil, for example, has already brought considerable wealth and gross inflation to Nigeria, and has caused the West to take a different view of that country's importance. Should oil be discovered in large quantities in the Sahara, for example, it will most certainly mean that countries there will become the focus of world interest. At present copper is very low priced on the world market, and this single factor has had disastrous effects upon Zambia's economy, but totally external factors could completely change this situation and thus refloat Zambia's economy and increase her interest to the West. Future patterns in the manufacture of civil and military aircraft, for example, may increase the demand for bauxite (made into aluminium) which is mined in Ghana and Jamaica. Clearly the increasing world demand for crude oil will make it the most significant and sought after mineral deposit in this decade, and countries that are able to export this vital mineral will find themselves able not only to command a very high price for it, but also to dictate the terms under which they will sell it. Indeed it seems quite likely that to be a major exporter of oil, even though they may have to import expatriate personnel and machinery to drill it, may put some countries' membership of the Third World in question. As Dudley Seers has suggested, there has been a growing fuzziness in the boundary between the 'developed' and 'developing' countries. How does one classify Kuwait, which has the highest per capita income in the world? It would be absurd to regard Kuwait as 'more developed' than the USA, so what are the norms of 'underdevelopment' or 'developing'? Dudley Seers suggests a new method of 'dependency classification' comparing the degree of self-sufficiency in technology, cereals and oil. These new norms have not been generally accepted by development economists yet, but his suggestions certainly merit careful thought.[8]

Secondly, the Third World will increasingly attract world interest – for all sorts of reasons. Some of these may be purely altruistic, others will certainly not be. As we have seen in the paragraph above, one 'magnetic factor' is, and will continue to be, raw materials and fuel needed to support the economy of both Western and Eastern blocs. Another will be concerned more with power politics – both West and East want to build good relationships with the Third World, partly for economic reasons, but as much for motives of power-competition; if we don't, you will! One very significant illustration of this is the increasing Russian-Cuban involvement in East and Central Africa. Starting with the coup in Zanzibar in 1964, Russian or Cuban influence has been felt in Angola, in Mozambique, in training freedom fighters for the final onslaught on the apartheid regime in S. Africa, and has already been evidenced in Ethiopia. This is not to imply that Western influences have been lacking – Callaghan's visit to President Kaunda in 1978, for example, could perhaps have been seen as an attempt by Britain to maintain her influence in Central and Southern Africa. Similarly, it will be interesting to see the extent to which India, Pakistan or indeed any Third World country might become focal centres of political interest on the part of both Western and Eastern powers in the future, for whatever reasons that interest is engendered.

Thirdly, the continuing dominance of the USA in Third World affairs will obviously influence development and thinking in many areas. Although perhaps Carter's strenuous attempts to produce a peace formula between Egypt and Israel in 1977–78 were not directly related to the Third World, they do illustrate America's ongoing and very deep interest in the world scene. American involvement in Vietnam was one prime example of this interest, and the Reagan administration gives every indication of pursuing a strong line in many parts of the Third World. American aid to the Third World in 1980 was £3,550 million, as compared to the British figure of £900 million, and although in terms of percentage of these two countries' GNP, the British figure was 0.34% compared to USA's 0.27%, in terms of cash actually spent in the Third World, the American figure is much greater. Aid, for whatever motives it has been given, does buy influence, and American influence in the Third World, whether exercised through skilled technical personnel, large scale marketing arrangements, or even through Christian missionaries, should not be underestimated.

In many ways one would wish to insulate the Third World from all these external influences and allow the countries of Africa, Asia, South America and the Caribbean to plot their own courses for development and, to some extent at least, to work out their own salvation. But this is an impossible dream; the realities are rather that we are living in one world, albeit a very unequal one and in some ways becoming more unequal. And interaction between the equal and unequal parts will continue, and will continue to be more complex in the next decade.

So what of the next ten years in the Third World? Leaving aside pointless crystal-ball gazing, we can be certain that development *will* continue. As a group, the under-developed countries achieved a growth rate of 5% per annum in their GDP for the Development Decades (1960–79). This figure will most probably be raised in the early '80s. As we have already seen (page 20) there are snags in statistics, and the figure of 5% quoted above is reduced to 2.3% when considered in *per capita* terms – and even this figure cannot tell us anything about the *distribution* of that income among the population.

Yet development is occurring, and will continue to do so; unevenly, with unexpected stops and starts and with some individual experiments like that of Tanzania. Some of these experiments may succeed, while others will probably fail.

Fourthly, development in the Third World will be *planned*. The extent to which Governments plan, and what form this planning takes, varies considerably: the spectrum ranges from Cuba at one extreme to Thailand and the Philippines at the other. But they all plan. There may be a State master plan like the Development Plans in Russia in the '30s and in many African countries in the '60s and '70s, or rather a series of measures directed at particular areas, like nationalization of expatriates' farms or fierce tariff protection of new industrial development. The State may take over more and more economic and social activities to ensure that they operate efficiently. Government planning will probably be *authoritarian* rather than *permissive*, simply because a laissez-faire policy has not worked so far. But it is a safe guess to predict that planning, in one form or another, will be an increasingly common factor of Third World development.

Another certain development in the Third World is the increasing growth of cities with all the consequent problems this entails. There are already 100 million more inhabitants living in cities in the Third World than in the rest of the world, and about 100 Third World cities already have a population of over one million people. It is reckoned that by 1985 there will be 414 cities with a population of over one million people, of which 276 will be in the Third World.[9] The six largest growing cities in the world can be found in the Third World, and this general trend will continue. These statistics taken in isolation may appear far less ominous than in fact they are, because whereas in Europe cities developed *in response to* the new forces of undustrialism, and people moved to the new industrial towns in the late eighteenth and early nineteenth centuries because the work was waiting for them, this has not been the case in the Third World. The people have indeed come to the towns to find work, but they have been unsuccessful. In Brazil, for example, in 1960 the proportion of urban dwellers was 28.1%, but only 9.5% of Brazil's population were working in industry – the rest were either grossly underemployed or completely without work.

This kind of problem will increase. As the differences between rich and poor are contrasted more sharply in the cities than in the countryside, 'so the expanding cities will be the tinder boxes of tomorrow's conflicts' (quoted in an article by Harold Davies in *Sunday Times*, 11th February 1973). Perhaps the outbreaks of inner city unrest in Britain in 1981, may serve to remind us of some of these dangers. In the eighties more people will flock to the cities to find work, will be disappointed and frustrated, but will find the cost of living much higher there than in the rural areas, and will quickly turn to crime to enable them to make ends meet. Another problem will be the moral one; unemployed adolescents will force up the illegitimacy rate and prostitution will flourish. The total problem is aggravated by the flourishing tourist trade that often exists in these large cities. I remember being very saddened by the disagreeable contrast between the sophisticated, entertainment-orientated area of Kingston (Jamaica) where the tourists stayed, and the appalling slums of nearby shanty town West Kingston. This situation can be found in so many Third World cities today – Nairobi, Bangkok, Buenos Aires and Delhi are obvious examples. Not only do tourists go home from their tropical holidays with a totally wrong impression of the Third World city scene, but also their presence exacerbates the division between rich and poor, and therefore the anger and frustration felt by the poor towards the rich minorities.

This is an unhappy picture, and one of which many Governments are only too well aware. Several countries (e.g. Tanzania, Zaïre) have forced unemployed young people to go back to the villages, and some have instituted a kind of 'pass' system which forbids youngsters to come and live in the cities unless they can produce evidence of a job to go to. But urban unrest will unfortunately be a 'running sore' in the Third World for the forseeable future.

Politically, it would seem to be almost inevitable that unstable conditions will persist, and this will probably mean that regimes that have allowed themselves to become economically corrupt will be toppled, sometimes by a military organised coup or by a purist group within the country. This has been the pattern so far in many countries in both Africa and Asia – there have been coups in Ghana, Nigeria, Sierra Leone, Ethiopia and Pakistan for example, and the Gandhi regime in India has come under severe attack for alleged corruption.

Before being quick to criticize these countries for their political instability, we need to remind ourselves that Western style democracy is a new and relatively untried system of government in the Third World. Previous to colonial rule, government was much more localised, usually tribal and extending over a much smaller area. In the case of India and Pakistan, authoritarian monarchical rule was made effective by means of local royal officials. In all cases government was strong, usually through an individual, and the people were content to follow. Concepts of 'government by the people, for the people and through the people', although perhaps the ideal form in the West, are still being adapted to local situations, and sometimes this process of adaptation is a painful one.

One interesting Third World variation on the theme of democracy is that of one-party government. It is seen by some critics as the prelude to Russian-style authoritarianism, but this is an inaccurate analysis. It may rather be seen as a fusion of Western democratic systems and the traditional forms of strong, individualised government. President Nyerere, for example, has argued that a country like Tanzania, with an urgent need for economic and social development, has no place for an organised opposition. Which party would set out to *oppose* the country's development? Surely it would make more sense for *all* parties to join together to form a single group and to work together for their national good!

There are some in this country who would argue that there might be a lesson for us to learn, as we tire of politicians' wrangles while the economy appears to worsen daily. Of course the expedient of one-party rule is dangerous, in that it can easily be used as a ploy to stifle any independent political thinking, as happened under the Amin regime in Uganda and appeared to have happened under Bhutto in Pakistan, and one hopes that the one-party regime is seen as a temporary expedient. But in contemporary Africa and Asia it should not be regarded as ipso facto totalitarian.

There may well be some Christian writers and thinkers who would have reservations about these last two paragraphs, and argue that we are witnessing a number of tyrannical regimes in the contemporary Third World. They cite not only Amin's bloody regime in Uganda but also a number of other regimes in Africa and Asia that have held power by force. There are valid arguments in their favour: many new nations have gone through periods of 'strong' government – and the word 'strong' is indeed used euphemistically. But the writer still holds to his view that the One Party State should not be regarded as ipso facto tyrannical, and that military regimes are not necessarily totally evil.

Finally, a point already made frequently in this chapter, Third World countries will continue to be jealous of their independence and sensitive to outside interference. They may decide to become completely identified with one 'super power' or another, but will do so for their own reasons, and may react violently if their support has been courted for motives of self-interest. True, external pressures, and in some cases military force, may be so great that a country succumbs involuntarily, as happened in Cambodia and Korea, but my guess is that this situation will not happen too frequently, and countries in the Third World will continue to try to take their own stances on major issues.

All this is highly relevant for missionary strategy, and the point will be considered further in the next chapter. But should *we* not be equally aware of these national areas of sensitivity? It does matter that we begin to understand what makes the Third World 'tick' if we are to follow the strategies of our chosen missionary society intelligently, or if we are to make sensible conversation with the overseas students we've invited to our home for the weekend, or whom we may meet professionally. So it is to be hoped that the factual input of this chapter will have been both intellectually digestible and practically useful.

Perhaps we should conclude this chapter by reiterating a point made at the beginning and on several occasions in the last forty pages. The Third World is indeed a very complex area to analyse, and if the reader turns over to the next page with an impression only of poverty, deprivation and overall human wretchedness, he (or she) has not received the message intended.

Indeed there is poverty, but there is also uneven wealth; there is hunger and some affluence and even ostentation. Indeed, the task of categorising becomes more difficult each day. If the model for a Third World country includes chronic unemployment, serious inflation and balance of payment difficulties, what about West Europe – or even Britain? What about Kuwait? New jargon is being invented in an attempt to clarify the situation. NICs (newly industrialising countries) and some of the richer members of OPEC countries must clearly now be distinguished from the poorer low income countries and Dudley Seers argues for a new look at the dimensions of dependence.[10]

It is not unlikely that some Third World countries will move from one World Bank League to the next – i.e. from Low Income Countries to Middle Income Countries, and the gap between the very poor and the more fortunate will get wider.

But there is still a lot of poverty in the Third World, much human suffering, dreadful unemployment and illiteracy remains high. And our Lord has given us a command to 'give them something to eat' (Mark 6:37). Let us never lose sight of that divine command as we try to gain a reasoned view of the Third World.

But what about the church in the Third World? Is it poor and wretched? Is it weak and lifeless? The next chapter will attempt to offer some interesting and perhaps exciting material which should dispel that impression.

3

The Changing Missionary Scene

This chapter has not been an easy one to write. Firstly, interviews with missionary societies have of necessity been selective. I have wanted to illustrate the principles underlying change by means of case studies, but thereby one runs the risk that the sample one selected was not a proper one. Secondly, I would have liked a much greater input from Third World church leaders, and this has been very difficult to organise because of the impersonal constraints of correspondence. I would have liked to have travelled round the world and talked to national church leaders as well as members of the laity, but for obvious reasons this was not possible. Thirdly, should I allow the dichotomy between 'mission' and 'national church' by treating these two subjects in separate chapters? Is there a 'hidden curriculum' implied here? The reason for the division is the overall constraint of length; news of the church in the Third World is so refreshing that it merited a chapter on its own.

But it has been a satisfying chapter to write; a number of missionary societies are 'on the move', and there is a growing awareness of the need to change to adapt to a rapidly changing Third World scene. What is less certain is the extent to which this comment may also be made of man in the pew.

In the first place, what is our perception of 'mission'? The Lord's final commission to his disciples before leaving them to return to his Father has in no way been revoked. Today, as in those exciting days when the church was born, we should 'go to all peoples everywhere and make them my disciples' (Matt 28:19). Two thousand years later, man is still separated from God because of his sin, and still needs to hear the Christian Gospel assuring him that God has done what man could never do for himself by sending his Son to pay the penalty for our sin in our place. Men and women, whatever their culture or sociological background, can turn from their sin and enjoy a restored relationship with God as sons and daughters of a living Father, by claiming for themselves the forgiveness made possible by the finished work of Christ at Calvary. And the Lord still expects his followers to communicate this glorious message to those who 'sit in darkness and in the shadow of death'.

That message hasn't changed; the Gospel is still the Good News, and it does still transform the lives of men and women who will receive it. But the medium may have changed, and indeed the strategies that we may use to communicate the Gospel have also changed. But before we consider methods, what do we understand by that well loved phrase in evangelical parlance, 'the mission field'? Or missionary societies? Or indeed, what is happening to missionaries themselves in the 1980s?

WHAT DO WE MEAN BY 'MISSION FIELD?

What is our perception of the 'mission field'? Images of the kind white missionary talking talking to a group of smiling black semi-clad children still persist, and these images may well be reinforced by some of the missionary magazines we read. Indeed, some of the names of missionary societies – The Unevangelised Fields Mission; The Regions Beyond Missionary Union; – may in part reinforce this image. Perhaps more significantly, some missionaries on deputation seem to major in recounting their experiences of a rather *primitive*, rather *exotic* mission field, telling us of the appalling roads they have to traverse in order to reach a church in some remote part of wherever. And no doubt those stories are true, even if at times they do get slightly embellished in the telling! After all, some missionaries do live and work in remote areas; their work *does* consist of helping pastors or running clinics in areas where national Christian workers are perhaps reluctant to serve. Because this is a factor that must be taken into account when placing an expatriate missionary; often national Christian workers, who may have been educated in the capital city or in one of the larger towns, are very reluctant to go and live in areas where the normal comfort and convenience amenities are lacking. We must not forget also that there are still many thousands of people in many parts of the Third World who have never heard the name of Jesus Christ. Indeed, the final address at the EMA Annual Conference (1979) given by Dr Ralph

Winter, General Director of the US Centre for World Mission, was devoted to a discussion of 'the unreached people' in the Third World who have not yet established any formal church. Although Dr Winter's figure of 16,700 'hidden churchless tribes' was challenged by a number of delegates from British missionary societies at that conference, there are still many peoples who have never heard the Gospel, and still more who have not established churches within their boundaries.

But, as we have already made clear in Chapter Two, it would be quite wrong to regard the 'mission field' and 'primitiveness' as synonymous, and ignore the complexity and contrasts within the Third World. One sometimes regrets that missionaries are not more careful to offer their listeners a more balanced overview of the country in which they are working. Perhaps if they were more aware of the overall ignorance of the Third World in the pew, and of the image of 'primitive Africa' or 'heathen India' that still persists in the Christian constituency, they would take more pains to present a balanced picture consistently when speaking on missionary delegation platforms. One African student studying at London Bible College described the increasing embarrassment he and his fellow-Africans felt on one occasion when a missionary visiting the College to talk about his work with a particularly primitive tribe, showed a set of slides illustrating the life-style of this backward people. This student made the point that, although he was well aware of the primitive life-style of the tribe amongst whom the missionary worked, he wished that he had prefaced his talk by showing a few slides of a more sophisticated Africa, if only to correct any inbalanced picture the English students present might have gained of his own home country. And are not missionary societies aware that often congregations are inclined to dig their hands more deeply into their pockets if they could feel that their stewardship was helping *'to hold the ropes'* in these *'darkest areas'* (the italics are mine!). Perhaps a missionary announcing his return to live in a modern fifth floor flat in Nairobi to work among young people in the inner city area, or to minister to students in the University, would find people more reluctant to give generously. They might be even *more* reluctant if he has accepted an invitation to become a pastor of Nairobi Baptist Church.

(It should be stated here that there is a Baptist Church in Nairobi and that it has called expatriates, including Rev Tom Houston and Dr Roy Clements and Gottfried Osei-Mensah [a

Ghanaian] to its pastorate. The Church is totally independent of mission funds and control, and exercises a key ministry in perhaps the most important city in East Africa. It has a congregation and a diaconate that is multi-racial and attracts students, senior civil servants and business men, as well as a cross-section of Nairobi working people. In the traditional, often accepted sense, Nairobi Baptist Church is not in a 'missionary' situation, but in the scriptural sense, it most certainly is!). Today therefore, as well as serving the church in rural areas, missionaries also work in large cities. The Church Missionary Society, for example, has eight families based in Nairobi, three of whom are in professional posts serving the church in Kenya. CMS also provide a pastor for a city church in Karachi, and for another city church in Freetown. The latter is also industrial chaplain to the city and his wife teaches at the Theological College. The Baptist Missionary Society has five workers in Dacca, the capital of Bangladesh, four in Delhi and twelve in Kinshasa (1979). Similarly other societies have expatriate personnel working in the rapidly growing cities of the Third World, whose lifestyle would be totally different from that of many missionaries today, or indeed of any 'old style' missionaries recruited thirty years ago. It may well be that in the next twenty years these mushrooming cities will become priority areas for expatriate missionaries to offer their skills in accountancy, architecture or management – a far cry from the 'bush missionary' of a previous generation.

Of course we in Britain are also living in a very needy mission field. In addition to the 50 million natives who were born here, there are approximately two million men and women of other cultures and traditions who have come to make their homes in this country. We find that we do not have to join a missionary society and travel halfway round the world in order to minister to Hindus, Muslims or Sikhs – they may well be living in the next street. Not that that fact alone necessarily makes the communication process much easier; perhaps more churches in multi-ethnic areas need to offer some form of background information and training that will facilitate the bridge-building process. All Nations Christian College might well provide excellent orientation courses for those preparing for mission service *overseas*; but don't those of us who live in multi-ethnic Birmingham or Brent also need some help if we are to be missionaries to our neighbours, about whose way of life we know so little?[1]

Some missionary societies have appreciated this new and very immediate area of mission, among them CMS, BCMS, and BMMF. CMS have appointed a Community Relations Secretary to carry out a programme of Church education. Bernard Nicholls, who held that post in 1979, wrote in the CMS Report *Together in Mission*:

> I have seen clergy and laity quietly getting on with long-term loving in the most appalling adverse circumstances....One of the sadder aspects has been the discovery that in some cases, only a short distance from a city twilight area with a concentration of immigrants, there are 'comfortable' suburban parishes apparently unaware of the other situation. There is sometimes an acute contrast between missionary interest in affluent parishes, focused on somewhere several thousand miles away, and the apparent indifference to the missionary situation only a few miles away.

In 1982 the Evangelical Race Relations Group (ERRG) appointed its first full-time worker, with the object of educating the churches toward a Christian understanding of race and also working towards a better understanding between the mainline denominations and the black churches. The International Christian Fellowship, the Red Sea Mission team and WEC also have some involvement in this area of mission.

Another body recently set up to bring the gospel of Christ to Asians living in London is 'In Contact'. Based in a redundant vicarage, church and schoolrooms in East London, 'In Contact' is concerned with church-planting in an inner city area with a considerable Asian population. Their projects include a Christian bookshop/Counselling Centre designed for Asians, and a church established among the Bengali community in Whitechapel. Altogether nineteen full-time workers are involved in 'In Contact'; some of these are young people who offer a period of several months to this work, while others are older men with professional skills. The team is led by Patrick Sookhdeo.

So perhaps we need to rethink our rather traditional and perhaps outdated concept of the mission field, and widen our horizons to appreciate something of the complexity of the contemporary Third World scene, as well as gain a new awareness of the immediate proximity in many of our large towns of those for whom the Gospel is as strange as to any living 3000 miles away. And the list of 'totally ignorant' will include many young people who have been born and reared in this country, and who are as English as the rest of us!

MISSIONARY SOCIETIES

But what about missionary societies? Perhaps it is at this point that some of us might find ourselves slightly on our guard, lest there be any suggestion that the favourite society we have for many years faithfully supported be proved in any way wanting!

It is something of a truism to suggest that perhaps there are too many of them. There are 71 UK based missionary societies in the Evangelical Missionary Alliance, and this number excludes a number of main-line non-conformists societies (Baptist Missionary Society, Methodist Church – Overseas Division, Council for World Mission, London Missionary Society and Presbyterian Church of England Overseas Mission). Over 40 member societies of the EMA attended the Annual Conference held at High Leigh in November 1978, and there were 49 at the 1981 Conference. Peter Brierley in the EMA Protestant Missions Handbook lists 82 societies with offices in this country that send British personnel overseas. 61 of these societies have less than 50 total serving members in this country. There are approximately 90 missionary publications produced on a regular basis, some monthly. To handle all the administration required to distribute these 90 magazines etc. approximately 900 office staff are employed in addition to 445 executive staff.[2]

One appreciates the historical background to the present multiplicity of missionary societies and also the obstacles that would have to be overcome, in terms of reassuring supporters as well as missionaries, if some programme of amalgamation were to be suggested. But one is less sympathetic when one realises that even a limited programme of sharing administration facilities has been quite difficult to 'sell'. In fact the EMA handbook for 1977 records only 15 societies that are working in some form of administrative cooperation, or (in about 6 cases) have totally amalgamated. When one takes into account the considerable duplication of administrative expenditure here at home, (manning and maintaining 70 sets of offices, 90 mailing lists for 90 magazines, financing 70 mission boards and selection procedures etc.), not to mention the difficulties experienced overseas, where not only those 70 British societies but also the much larger number of North American and European groups have established *their* systems, *their* liturgy and *their* idiosyncracies – *then* one wonders whether the need for some programme of coordination of resources, if not amalgamations, is not more immediate than 'respecting individuals' preferences and reasons of history'. Maintaining a UK office is an expensive item in the '80s; although a number of societies have moved out of Central London – the departure of the Overseas Missionary Fellowship from Newington Green to Sevenoaks must have seemed like the end of an era to some missionary veterans! Societies reckon to devote more than 20% of their budget to UK expenses. Although Tear Fund is proud to report that their UK administrative costs are less than 15%, the total UK costs for the 7 Anglican Missionary Societies in 1976 (and this figure included their total education programme in this country) was £1,550,000 out of a total income of £4,600,000 – approximately 34%. Not only is a sizeable proportion of *finance* earmarked for maintaining the home base; whereas in the four years 1966–70 the total number of missionaries recruited by British societies declined by 20% (and that decline has continued throughout the 70s) the number of home-based personnel involved in administration, deputation and fund-raising doubled from 5–10% of the total mission force in that same period. The CMS reported that in 1976, 128 of their staff were homebased out of a total of 410 – a figure of 31%! Nor is this an isolated statistic; the EMA handbook indicates that in the same year 1,341 personnel working with mission were UK based and 4,147 were either abroad or on furlough. Thus 32% of all mission personnel were home based in 1976!

Indeed, this brief and incomplete survey of the contemporary UK mission scene makes it abundantly clear that some form of cooperation at home is long overdue. To set the records straight, some societies have realised this fact. In 1981 a long-cherished dream of some founder-members of the executive of the EMA was realised. Six societies, four of them working overseas and two in this country, came together to purchase a large modern building in South East London with the express view of sharing their UK based administrative backup, and also to work towards a closer form of amalgamation. Whitefield House in Kennington houses the British arm of the Bible and Medical Missionary Fellowship, the Regions Beyond Missionary Union, the Andes Evangelical Mission and the Evangelical Union of South America (these two last-mentioned societies have amalgamated in everything but name already), the Church Society and the Evangelical Alliance. The six share a common reception area, a joint office for the storing of data, and a computer to facilitate their financial transactions as well as modern recording studios for the production of audio-visual resource material. The societies concerned recognise that this move may well to some extent mute their identity, but believe that the move will be both cost-effective and helpful to the general image of missionary societies as perceived by the churches.

One can only applaud this form of rationalisation of resources, in that it not only releases financial resources for work in the Third World but also provides a more efficient servicing agency for all concerned. One hopes that this will become a 'pilot scheme' to be followed by other groups of missionary societies sharing similar interests in the future.

The EMA has in fact for some time been working hard behind the scenes to bring missionary societies closer together. One very practical instance of EMA-sponsored cooperation has been the formation of three regional groups within its membership for Latin America, Africa and Asia. The former two groups have produced a single publicity/recruitment brochure, listing the member societies and their future personnel needs. Arthur Pont, Chairman of EMA, commented that there has been some movement in the direction of inter-mission cooperation in recent years, but he also spoke of 'some disenchantment' as the problems encountered in drawing societies together seem so unnecessarily complicated! The annual EMA conference also brings societies together once a year 'to think mission', but it seems that we need to go further than that in the '80s.

There are indeed some promising indications of a greater willingness to cooperate, but these signs are very recent.

There are still a lot of small missionary societies with a UK administrative base, and as costs soar, and also as it becomes increasingly difficult to recruit overseas mission personnel of the 'long-term' variety so it becomes increasingly imperative that the resources that are available are used to the optimum advantage, and serve best the new national churches in the Third World.

Ernest Oliver, founder-secretary of the EMA and a missionary thinker whose views are widely respected in Britain and the Third World, has suggested that missionary societies should be working towards a Tear Fund style of structure. They should be more project orientated, concerned to service the national churches rather than to perpetuate their own existence.

Having made this point, however, there are some very encouraging developments to report in terms of a changing missionary strategy and also changing relationships with national churches. This is a key issue, as Great Britain and her former colonial territories enjoy a very different kind of relationship from that which pertained when missionary societies were first established. A further comment will be made about this a little later in the chapter. It may be of value first to consider briefly other aspects of changing missionary society policy. What about mission publicity methods, for example? The heady days of the 'May meetings', when night after night the Central Hall, Westminster, was packed with supporters of this or that society thrilling to the testimonies of outgoing recruits, are no longer part of the mission scene. There are missionary meetings, but these tend to be held regionally and have somewhat changed format. In 1979, for example, the Sudan United Mission held some sixteen regional halfday or day conferences, as well as a London annual meeting and two Keswick camps and young people's holiday houseparties. CMS had a similar programme, but in addition planned a British tour of the Ugandan Bishop Festo Kivengere and organised an Open Day at their London Headquarters. This event was cancelled at the last moment because Bishop Kivengere was called back to Uganda following the overthrow of Idi Amin. He returned to speak in Britain in 1981. Scripture Union capped it with a centenary thanksgiving service in St. Paul's Cathedral in 1979, but they have for some time concentrated on regional meetings, many taking the form of 'workshop sessions' with teachers and youth workers.

Most societies recognise that the 'one night stand' of mission deputation is the least effective method of publicity and education. It is expensive and often chancy – a missionary albeit a popular one, visiting a church for a single evenings deputation, may well suffer from the competition of a top-rating TV serial! Missionary societies prefer to organise *regional* deputation programmes, when two or three missionaries can be based in a town for a couple of weeks and work to a programme organised by the local churches in active cooperation. But this strategy, although ideal, depends upon a considerable degree of cooperation from the local churches, and unfortunately this is not often the case. Obviously when a missionary is known to his church he is likely to command better support, but even this is not always assured. Churches seem to become so immersed in the immediate situation or crisis that a missionary overseas for two or three years tends to get forgotten.

One very interesting, and indeed a forward-looking experiment in mission deputation, was conducted in S. E. London in the Autumn of 1979. Three societies, RBMU, Missionary Aviation Fellowship and Wycliffe Bible Translators, staged a combined operation as part of the Rye Lane Baptist Church, Peckham, missionary week. The emphasis was on *total mission involvement* in Irian Jaya rather than on the input of the three individual societies, and listeners were able to get some idea of the considerable degree of inter-mission cooperation that exists in that country, appreciating the degree to which MAF services missionary societies and Wycliffe Bible Translators works alongside them. More, the impact of this 'in-depth look' was considerably increased by a number of short, well-chosen slide-tape sequences, and by the informality of the chairman, who conducted a series of interviews with missionaries and home-based staff, rather than presiding over a series of monologues. Spontaneous questions were invited from the audience as the meetings proceeded, and one felt that interest was maintained throughout the sessions and a much more accurate overview given of mission work in Irian Jaya than would have been possible in three separate happenings, organised by three separate societies.

Perhaps this is the way for the future. Should not *individual* missionary societies do better to seek to maintain a low profile, and rather to bring into sharper focus the church of Jesus Christ in another part of the world, if at all possible sharing their platforms with national church leaders?

Quite a number of societies have moved into the 'hardware' market, producing slide-tape sets or sound strips for loan to churches and housegroups, describing a missionary's work or illustrating work in a particular country. EMA runs an annual communications course, designed to help missionaries on furlough etc. to maximise the use of their audio-visual materials and to think more carefully about the skills of communication and, equally important, what are *their objectives* while on deputation. The number of missionaries who still rely on incidents recounted from the pulpit or who insert their slides upside down into the projector is too large to be quoted! The faithful missionary magazine still continues, albeit in new and abbreviated format – but this change merely reflects trends that cover the complete spectrum of Christian activity in the '80s. We hear less often of the missionary exhibition: I can still vividly remember one held in my London church in 1948, when different societies spread their wares on a long line of trestle tables in the church hall. And

what a marvellous collection of artefacts they managed to display!
Cowrie shells, gourds, Gospels written in strange languages,
photographs of missionaries on the job – the lot! But they did the
trick – they caught the imagination of young Christians and
there was no shortage of missionary recruits in the '50s.

Missionary finance is still an all too common problem – or to be
more specific, the lack of it. In December 1980 *Crusade* ran a
leader-article 'Missions in Crisis'. It revealed that, of the twenty
or so missionary societies that revealed their financial position,
thirteen reported a shortfall of income against budgeted or actual
expenditure in 1979-80 of between 2% and 16%. In some cases
the deficit was made up by drawing upon bank reserves, but in
others missionaries' salaries were cut, projects curtailed or aban-
doned, and vacancies had to remain unfilled. On the other hand
some societies did in fact go for a growth budget and reported
increased giving, but this is in no way keeping up with the
continuing inflation in UK, let alone the higher inflation in some
Third World countries. Ghana, for example, has inflation running
at 160% annually and Argentina 260%. And even these figures
do not give a realistic analysis of the rate of inflation in some
Third World countries, because often there simply isn't the currency available to buy the goods! Thus one missionary in an
article of 1978 on his work as a doctor in a remote area of Zaïre,
captioned his piece 'If only We Had', and goes on to report one
conversation with a hospital administrator concerning the purchase of a 50 gallon drum of petrol which at £150 was regarded as
a bargain! Even the increased giving to the BMS in 1977-8 of 19%
(and this is no mean increase) could not hope to cope with that
degree of inflation. Other problems that arise when countries like
Zaïre suffer from hyper-inflation cause some heart-searching;
should missionary societies, for example, allow their workers to
buy currency 'on the black market', where they would get a much
better exchange rate, or stick to the official channels? When a
currupt port official at Lagos or Bombay could so successfully be
'persuaded' to streamline a missionary's personal effects through
customs for a few naire or rupees, *should* a missionary spend
valuable days sitting at customs control going through the proper
official channels, or should he not reckon his time to be sufficiently valuable to the country he is serving to idemnify his
conscience and pay the bribe?

A number of societies have organised special funds to raise
money for specific projects, either for some kind of crisis relief or

for some project that may appeal as well to the heart as to the head. 'Operation Agri' is a fund devised by the BMS to finance projects with an agricultural bias – a well to enable a school in Delhi to grow its own vegetables, a fruit and vegetable farm in Panama, and so on. Although 'Operation Agri' has caught on in Baptist Churches and many have replaced the traditional harvest marrows with a special 'Agri' envelope, the scheme has the slight disadvantage in that monies given to 'Operation Agri' cannot be released for other purposes. This has meant that there have been occasions when BMS has needed funds for its general support needs and has not been able to release the monies in the 'Agri' fund. Some missionary societies are rather concerned about this growing trend in missionary giving. They report that the Christian constituency seems much more willing to give to an interesting project like building a new school or providing piped water than to the ongoing pastoral work of a faceless missionary.

TEAR FUND

Tear Fund also makes special appeals to help send relief in times of natural crisis, like the floods in India or earthquakes in Iran. In 1979, the International Year of the Child, they devoted an issue of their magazine (*Tear Times*) to 'The World's Most Valuable Resource – the Child', and *Tear Topics* published at the same time, spelled out the hazards facing many children living in the Third World – malnutrition, brain damage, incomplete education etc., and concluded with details of their Short-Term sponsorships, a scheme designed to help teenage children living in Third World cities to have some education. Tear Fund has a Department of Child Care, and in cooperation with an American organisation 'Compassion' has launched a very successful 'sponsor a child' programme.

Tear Fund is certainly in business; founded in 1968 as a separate relief agency, although with roots firmly grounded in its parent body, The Evangelical Alliance, its income in its first year of operation was £2,687, in 1978-9 £2.0 million and in 1979-80 £3.27 million. The idea for Tear Fund can be said to have originated in The Year of the Refugee 1959, when Evangelical Christians, among others, felt that they had a responsibility to give needy refugees but wanted to channel their contributions into some specifically Christian cause. Some sent money to the Evangelical

Alliance, therefore, and at their Executive Council in January 1960 the EA passed the following resolution:

> That in response to numerous requests the Evangelical Alliance should set up a fund whereby gifts could be distributed to evangelical agencies engaged in caring for the material and spiritual needs of refugees.

This fund, known as EAR (Evangelical Alliance Refugee) Fund was administered by George Hoffmann and was officially launched at a Press Conference on November 8th, 1968, when journalists were given lunch consisting of Rice Krispies, powdered milk and fruit served out of silver dishes! The fund was christened TEAR fund, with a motif of tear-shaped letters on a stark black and white image, and the Fund took as its first shock-tactic slogan 'They can't eat Prayer.' There is no doubt that Tear Fund has caught on in the evangelical scene. It has undoubtedly been helped by the personal support of Cliff Richard, who has visited a number of projects and has also performed in a number of Tear Fund concerts or recorded some soundstrips for them. Today it is a sizeable organisation with a UK staff of some 60 with eight separate departments – no mean growth from a file on the EA General Secretary's desk less than 15 years ago!

There have been occasional murmurings from missionary societies that their income has suffered because of Tear Fund's success. Undoubtedly many Evangelicals did feel that the missionary societies had failed to 'deliver the goods' in the '60s; they were not seen to be involved in the obvious and urgent needs of famine or national disaster relief, and their deputation workers were clearly not au fait with the rapidly changing Third World scene that was being mirrored on their TV sets. So Tear Fund gained from missionary societies' perceived failures, and a considerable number of Evangelicals gave to an organisation that was seen to be involved in caring, not just for the souls of men, but also for their physical needs.

Perhaps the unqualified success of Tear Fund indicates a radical change in evangelical thinking about mission and missionary societies in the last 10-15 years. There has certainly been a tendency in the past on the part of Evangelicals to shy away from matters that were labelled 'social involvement'. Mary Endersbee in the preface to her excellent story of Tear Fund – *They Can't Eat Prayer* puts the picture very succinctly:

> Mention the subject of evangelism and social involvement in the

same breath to some people, and you'll hear them mutter 'social gospel', 'compromise'. An out-of-date caricature? I don't think so. Many Christians today appear to have forgotten that Jesus Christ did not merely preach at people; he fed and healed them also. They seem to have forgotten as well the tremendous work done during the last century by Christians, many of them Evangelicals in public life, to improve the conditions of the destitute, the orphaned and the exploited.

Perhaps a certain disenchantment with the 'social gospel' is forgiveable. It has given the impression that we must be completely uninterested in the needs of men's souls. To avoid this lopsided approach, Evangelicals have swung to the opposite extreme. They have become so preoccupied with the needs of souls that they have tended to forget that men have also bodies.

Perhaps a further reason for the reluctance of British missionary societies to get too involved with the business of famine relief has been the extent of American influence still felt by some societies. Many British interdenominational societies have American branches and rely on considerable support from Christians in the USA, mainly in the 'Bible Belt' of the Southern States. Generally speaking, American missionary societies see their role in terms of evangelism, church planting and translation work, and feel relief work is of far less spiritual significance. And it may well be that some British societies have been influenced by this line of thought. But Tear Fund is one (and not the only) example of a missionary society that *is* involved in caring for the whole man – not seeking to catch his soul by giving him some free bread, but rather showing that the disciple of Jesus who is prepared to take his Lord's teaching seriously *must* equally show a concern for the least of his children who is hungry . . . or without clothes . . . or in prison (Matt. 25:35-40). Jesus himself on at least two occasions when faced with thousands of hungry people, told his disciples to give them something to eat. In the same way, missionaries of the eighties in a similar situation must feed the hungry, provided they don't regard a man's full belly as the quickest way to his soul, nor neglect to show him how to feed himself better in the future. And, equally important, so long as we do not begin to equate 'mission' with 'projects'. One missionary executive explained this point to me thus: 'Mission is still and must still be, the costly long term involvement of *people* with *people*. 'Nigel Sylvester, in an interview for the Centenary edition of Scripture Union's magazine made a similar point:

Question:What do you see as SU's role in the Third World?

Answer: Your use of the phrase 'the Third World' draws attention to the enormous physical need in many countries in Africa, Asia and Latin America, which Tear Fund, Oxfam etc. are so rightly stressing. When they see this sort of publicity, I think some people wonder if they should channel all their giving into relief work, because of our Christian care and concern. I think this needs to be kept in balance, because people do have spiritual needs as well as physical needs; they cannot live by bread alone, and as Christians we have a responsibility for them at both levels.

Another possible disadvantage of becoming too project-centred in one's planning concerns personnel. If a project depends too exclusively on one missionary, his departure or transfer may mean the end of an often uncompleted project.

CHANGING RELATIONSHIPS IN MISSION

So much for changing methods that missionary societies are adopting. But what about the more fundamental issue of their relationship with the local churches? Fifty years ago, missionary societies all had (more or less) prestigious offices in Central London. Wise, but usually older men sitting on committees sent missionaries to 'fields' across the seas. And those missionaries were expected to offer a life-time commitment – if someone quit after ten years, it was assumed that he had not fitted in very well on the field!

To illustrate the extent to which that picture has changed, I can do no better than quote at some length from a CMS publication, *Together in Mission '79*:

The Church Missionary Society, founded in 1799, has long since moved away from being solely a missionary-sending agency with a centre in London and 'fields' across the waters. Of course we still have missionaries: 349 working in 27 countries as diverse as Japan and the Yemen, with our heaviest committment in East Africa. We also have 76 volunteers, most but not all, young people, who go overseas for a year or more.

Fifty years ago CMS had nearly 1,200 missionaries many of whom staffed the extensive network of schools, colleges, hospitals and clinics in which most missionary societies invested heavily at the time. Through those institutions young churches were nurtured throughout the Empire and the contrast between those imperial days and

ours can be summed up in a couple of phrases – the Anglican Com-
munion and the new United Churches.

As last summer's Lambeth conference illustrated so vividly, York
and Canterbury are now simply two Anglican provinces among
twenty-five all on an equal footing and members one of another. But
there are no Anglican provinces in the Indian sub-continent. Instead,
praise God, we have the Church of South India, the Church of North
India and the new United Churches of Pakistan and Bangladesh.

Talk of the overseas mission field is only valid if we remember that
from God's point of view everywhere is 'overseas'. To an African
bishop, Britain's declining churches seem to languish in a 'heathen
land afar' and missionary societies must rapidly become two-way
channels through which we can all enrich each other.

It is no longer a question of 'We in Britain are sending to you in
the primitive and ignorant Third World who (or what) we decide
– we know what is good for you', but rather 'Share your needs
with us and we will see whether that part of the church of Christ
that functions in Britain can help you!'

It might help to illustrate this changing relationship between
the church in England and overseas by considering the pattern of
responsibility sharing of four societies; two quite large demoni-
national societies, the Baptist Missionary Society and the Church
Missionary Society; one large international organisation, Scripture Union International; and one smaller regionally based
society, the Sudan United Mission.

BMS's early missionaries were concerned to plant local churches and to associate themselves totally with the local Christians.
William Carey, their first missionary and virtually the founder of
the modern missionary movement, spent the first six years in
India working in an indigo factory and his first mission station at
Serampore was not established until he had learned the language
and knew something of [the] local culture. This policy was later
modified during the colonial period, when to some extent the
missionary was regarded (perhaps unfortunately) as part of the
colonial presence. Now they have gone back to their original
ideal, whereby missionaries are the servants of the local churches.
In fact BMS as an organisation does not exist anywhere else than
in this country – all missionaries identify totally with the local or
national church. Missionary personnel are placed by the local
Church in cooperation with both the BMS and the individuals
concerned. Their 'probation' is overseen both by the senior
missionary in that area and by the leaders of the local church.

After a period of furlough they return overseas at the specific request of the local church, and they may be moved from one station to another at the request of the same body. Many of the Baptist Churches in N. India have now joined the United Church of N. India, and this body has proposed that they seek to be independent of overseas personnel and financial aid by the '80s. Baptist Missionaries in Nepal are (by Government decree) members of the United Mission to Nepal with its headquarters in Khatmandu. Direct proselytization is forbidden, so there is no 'official' church and therefore deployment of mission personnel is undertaken by the United Mission of Nepal.

Thus decision making regarding missionary deployment within the fellowship of the BMS is a shared process. This inevitably takes longer than in the colonial days, and there are times when wisdom is needed, as, for example, when a local church in S. America decided to send its expatriate missionaries to remote areas with little chance of church building, basically because no national Christian would go there! As Rev A. S. Clement, the Home Secretary, confided to me – 'Life was more simple in the old days!' Missionary strategy today is of necessity more complex and time-consuming. But perhaps the extra time is well spent, if it facilitates the process of transfer of responsibility from London to the national churches.

CMS tells a similar story. They see themselves as an agency, linking overseas needs with British skills, and regard themselves rather as a 'resource bank', on the one hand receiving requests for Christians with specific needed skills, and on the other selecting and preparing possible candidates to fill the vacancies. CMS has quite a rigorous selection procedure, including a residential 'interview' at one of their diocesan centres, and all papers of candidates who are considered suitable for overseas posting are sent to the overseas church for their consideration. Once posted overseas, CMS missionaries become the employees of the local church, but also enjoy certain mission supports. For example, salaries are still paid by CMS (although each national church will make a contribution towards the mission staff working in the dioceses), CMS look after the education of their children and offer a pension scheme. Again like BMS, CMS are aware of 'the necessary constraints of partnership', and on some occasions *may* exert 'indirect pressure' when they feel that the world perspective that a London-based mission executive may have is of greater validity than a locally-based perception of a particular situation. But the General Secretary of CMS was emphatic in his comment that 'we never talk about the mission', and equally emphatically stressed that CMS is no longer in the plant-owning business; all plant, whether this be hospital, school or missionary housing, is now the property of the national church.

SCRIPTURE UNION INTERNATIONAL

Scripture Union International rather falls into a category of its own. It is a much larger society than most interdenominational societies, and it is not in the church planting business. Rather its objective is to serve the established churches by providing them with appropriate Bible reading aids, and also by offering a service to young people in schools and colleges. Yet the story of SU International provides a most interesting illustration of a new-style partnership between the old-style London based mission and Christian leaders in the Third World. Scripture Union in London celebrated its centenary Bible reading year in 1979, and is perhaps still known by some as CSSM, associated with holiday beach missions and children's choruses. This image would be a very inaccurate one today, however. Today SU has eight areas of commitment, including the provision of teaching materials for Sunday School teachers and youth group leaders, a growing Audio Visual Aids Department, providing a wide range of non-book material for use in house groups as well as more formal teaching situations, and also the production of a number of Bible reading aids. SU publishes a comprehensive range of books, and also works in schools (Inter Schools Christian Fellowship) and among inner city young people (Frontier Youth Trust).

SU International follows the same objectives. It coordinates an active SU presence in 85 countries, 64 of these in the Third World. It is even more exciting to report that these 40 countries bear the major responsibility, and in some cases also the financial support, for 151 staff workers, most of whom are nationals of the countries concerned. SU staff workers are engaged in a wide variety of activities. These include the promotion of Bible reading and distribution of Bible reading notes, which are mostly written by local writers; children's and young people's evangelism; training young people for leadership roles within SU groups in schools and colleges, and in some cases providing AVA materials. To take SU in Ghana as an example: the six Ghanaian staff workers visit groups in hundreds of secondary schools up and down the country, some of which may be in quite remote areas and desperately in need of fellowship, organise regional evangelistic rallies and camps for boys and girls at school, plan and speak at training seminars for leaders of SU groups, as well as liasing with the Africa Christian Press on the writing, printing and distribution of some 80 titles specifically written for an African readership. All the activities mentioned above are planned and run by nationals, often with expatriates acting as helpers in one form or another.

SU in Ghana offers almost a prototype of the manner in which a mission enterprise originally controlled and financed from London has now handed over both the reins of leadership and to a considerable extent financial responsibility to a locally based leadership, while still enjoying an excellent working relationship with the London body. In 1955, Nigel Sylvester, now Secretary of SU International, was appointed to promote SU activities in schools and colleges in Ghana, largely at the request of a number of expatriate school teachers and University lecturers working there in Government appointments. Later a local SU committee was set up, initially largely expatriate in membership but this quite quickly changed and Ghanaians formed the majority of members, most of whom were themselves in either academic or professional posts. The local committee gradually took over the reins of control, as well as assuming a large measure of financial responsibility. Thus when Culain Morris was appointed in 1967 to succeed Nigel Sylvester, this appointment was made by SU in Ghana, and Culain became an employee of that committee. More recently the many national committees in Africa (16 in 1978) together with 6 autonomous SU councils have themselves formed an African Regional Council, which has an overview of these National committees and has in its turn 3 full-time staff. They help with the practicalities of coordination (e.g. printing) and equally important looking after the physical distribution of SU notes and books. They also have a pastoral and advisory responsibility for SU staff throughout the continent. There are also Councils for Australia, S.E. Asia, S. Asia, Europe and the Middle East and the British Isles. In some cases, e.g. Australia and S.E. Asia, the wealthier members can help the poorer countries materially and in terms of manpower; but the vast majority of SU staff worldwide are nationals of the countries they are serving.

SU International's offices are in London but this is largely a matter of convenience, in the same way that the Commonwealth

Secretariat also has its offices in London. But London is neither the Headquarters of the Commonwealth nor of SU International! In many ways it makes sense for the office to be in London, partly because London is still the most convenient 'centre' and attracts most visitors, and also because of the important facility of the hundreds of charter flights that operate from London annually. In any case, SU International regards London as just as much the centre of the mission field as Nairobi, Buenos Aires or Onga Bonga! In fact a group of SU staff from Africa at present studying at All Nations Christian College constituted a mission team to S.E. England in 1978. One of the comments they made about the churches they visited was the apparent lack of serious interest in Bible study that they noticed. In 1979, two senior SU staff members from India and Africa toured parts of S.E. England, and this pattern of 'mission in reverse' is clearly one that SU intends to follow whenever possible.

So it would be quite wrong to regard SU International as a London promoted or controlled organisation. Perhaps the next Secretary will be a representative of the Third World. The International Council is convened in Third World countries from time to time. Already the Secretary's salary and travel expenses are paid on the basis of contributions from the five regional councils. (78-79 Budget – Africa 4%, Americas 5%, Australia and Far East 18%, Great Britain 37%, Europe 32%, India 2% and special gifts 2%). He sees his rôle partly as that of diplomat, advising where difficulties have arisen in one or another national Council, in part that of pastor – he is often invited to minister the Word to national or regional Councils. He is also regarded as one who can detect change in organizational emphasis and offer advice. He is in constant touch with a wide variety of committees, and hears as many views, so he does have the considerable advantage of having an overview of SU worldwide.

The story of SU International has been told in some detail, partly because it is an exciting one and also because it illustrates the direction in which one feels mission should be going. Increasingly control has moved from London to the Third World, but it is not thereby anticipated that Third World countries should lose the wealth of experience this country can offer, nor indeed reject the financial help or skilled personnel that are available and anxious to be 'lent' to the Third World. But London no longer holds the reins of control – and nor should it!

The organisational structure of SUM (Sudan United Mission)

is unlike that of most interdenominational societies in that, although it has worldwide support, it is not one large mission, with a single controlling committee laying down a policy for all branches to follow, but rather a fellowship of ten national branches, each operating autonomously. Thus the relationship between SUM and the church in Nigeria varies according to the country from which that particular branch of SUM operates. In 1977 a formal merger took place between SUM (British branch) and the Nigerian Church, and the Church of Christ in Nigeria became the new controlling body. Thus SUM missionaries became workers of the Church in Nigeria, and SUM (British branch) ceased to exist as a separate organisation. Recruitment of missionary personnel follows a similar pattern to that of CMS. Initial recruitment and selection is done from London, but quite early in this process papers are sent to COCIN (The Church of Christ in Nigeria), and once a candidate has been accepted, his posting is the responsibility of the local church. Again this process may take longer than the old fashioned 'London-directed' posting, but the principle is right. Missionaries' travel costs and stipends are paid from London, but their 'running costs' while in Nigeria (housing, language orientation) are paid to the Nigerian church for them to distribute. The Church has already expressed its desire to increase its contribution towards this capitation allowance, and thus to aim for financial independence from Great Britain.

Again in common with BMS and CMS, SUM also recruits short-term missionaries and associate missionaries, and these latter categories are usually appointed to fill specific posts that the church in Nigeria identifies. Also in common with CMS, SUM has handed over all its former plant in Nigeria to the Church. A Nigerian leader of COCIN wrote of the merger in these terms:

> By the grace of God a Church has been planted – the Church of Christ in Nigeria has come into being. All responsibilities which were hitherto carried by the Mission in Nigeria have been taken over by the Church. The Sudan United Mission (British Branch), which was instrumental in bringing the Church into being, ceased to be a separate organisation in Nigeria as from 1st January, 1977.
>
> From the enormous tasks and opportunities stated already, it is clear that the Church will continue to need the services of missionaries from overseas (inter-church workers) for as long as the Lord permits. The Church of Christ in Nigeria is a young and fast growing Church,

and because of her fast growing nature, she will continue to need all the help she can get for the ministries of evangelism, Bible teaching, leadership training and general building up. The Church leaders have stated explicity that they love, respect and want their missionary colleagues to continue to work in fellowship with the Church.

In the past, the SUM sent out missionaries to an unevangelised Nigeria. Now it is the Church that is requesting the Mission to send workers from the United Kingdom and Australia and New Zealand to help her. The expatriate workers who are now full members of the Church, will continue to serve the Lord Jesus and the Church using their gifts, training and experience for the building up of the body of Christ as Paul tells us in 1 Corinthians 12.

I have quoted at length from Rev Bitrus Pam's statement, because it well illustrates two important, and to my mind, very appropriate principles for mission in the '80s. On the one hand, the feeling of *national satisfaction* pervades the statement relating to the birth of the Church of Christ in Nigeria; on the other, a recognition of the fact that this same national church both *needs* and *welcomes* the involvement of expatriate workers, who now serve not at the direction of a board sitting in London, but rather as full members of the national church and under their directing.

Other societies report similar kinds of cooperation between the London base and the overseas church. The Administrative Secretary of RBMU wrote:

It has long been our objective that churches should become autonomous. We consider the situation in 'our' region of Zaïre to be fairly exemplary in that missionaries are sent only on the invitation of the regional church, to do work specified and monitored by them. Missionaries become members of the church and take their part in this process. Of course, their advice is listened to and often taken, but tact and respect are exercised on both sides. After a period in which Africans have been the figureheads, the stage has now been reached when top positions can now be occupied by missionaries purely on the grounds that he or she is the best person for a job; and is a member of the church.

A number of societies have moved their headquarters to the Third World. OMF moved to Singapore twenty years ago and more recently BMMF became a completely international mission, with final control in the hands of an international Council, consisting of two members from each of their five sending countries. BMMF's International Headquarters is in Delhi, but British expatriate missionaries are recruited by the London office and then placed by the Regional Superintendent.

Yet another case study of mission adapting to a different political environment is the United Mission to Nepal. The Government of Nepal has insisted that all Christian mission enterprise should be channelled through a single organisation based in the capital, Khatmandu. Thus the UMN was set up in 1954 and 28 missions (UK or USA based) send missionaries to fill specific posts. These are mainly related to educational or medical projects, but also to community development and rural development projects. Missionaries are not allowed to proselytise overtly, but there is clear evidence that there is a very live church in Nepal, and converts do not have to concern themselves regarding the choice of mission or denomination with which they associate – there is only the United Mission to Nepal (see pages 89–91).

All this makes exciting reading, and I found myself encouraged as I researched and wrote these last paragraphs. Indeed I found that I had to reappraise my own perceptions of mission as new and exciting changes in mission thinking began to emerge, and as I came to appreciate that some mission boards are making a serious effort to be more sensitive to the thinking and aspirations of the church in the Third World.

Two further comments are appropriate. Firstly, the extent to which this policy of amalgamation between mission and national church is really meaningful must depend to a very large extent on the attitudes of individual missionaries. If they are determined 'to get into the skin' of another culture – and this will mean not merely learning another language but also endless patience in listening to others and not being quick to impose a *British* solution to every problem – then the chances are that the theoretical linking of local church to mission society may become a reality. But if missionaries still take with them the package of attitudes and preconceptions that one still meets in so many of our churches, and still feel that they, or their society, has all the answers that the local church needs, or *ought* to need, then integration is no more than a piece of rather dishonest mission window dressing. Obviously there was no way in which I could discover the extent to which individuals are trying to adjust to this new situation, nor could I talk to African or S. American church leaders to ask them for their perceptions of missionaries' attitudes, but I did put the question to Dr Peter Cotterill, Director of Overseas Studies at London Bible College and author of *The*

Eleventh Commandment (IVP 1981), a study of biblical missiology.
His experience of students training at LBC with a mission career
very much in mind is that they are still totally unaware of the
changing Third World scene. He also felt that genuine parity on
an individual missionary to local church leader basis has not
been completely reached. His final comment I found very significant – 'missionaries need to have a much greater realisation that
the Holy Spirit is equally capable of guiding Third World church
leaders as London-based missionary boards.'

Patrick Sookhdeo presented a very thought-provoking paper
to the EMA Annual Conference in November 1979 entitled '*The
Response of the Younger Churches to the Western Missionary Movement*'. He made the point that, although there has been an
increasing amount of *talk* and the subsequent drawing up of
Declarations at International Missionary Congresses about partnership between Third World churches and Western missionary
societies, the Western Church still has a long way to go in
ridding itself of a colonial mentality, and in working positively
towards an attitude of interdependence with Third World
churches. He quoted a number of statements from Third World
church leaders reinforcing this viewpoint – one from South
America, a second from India and a third from Africa. In October
1978 at the second Quito consultation, the Bolivian Group issued
the following statement:

> We have come to this meeting with the desire to approach some
> problems of a neurotic nature in the Lord's work in our continent,
> and to seek, together with the representatives of foreign mission
> present here, solutions for those problems. However, after two days
> of discussion, we are under the impression that this objective isn't
> being reached. Because of this, we would like to pose the following
> questions, in hopes that they will serve as a channel for the delibera-
> tions of the final day of this consultation.
>
> 1. We question whether, up to now, there has been true dialogue
>   between the Latin Americans and the representatives of foreign
>   missions. We feel there has been only a monologue on the part of
>   the Latin Americans. In view of this, we ask: Have the mission
>   representatives really listened? Have they understood us? Have
>   they accepted what we've said up until now?
> 2. We would like the missionary personnel to, with complete honesty,
>   objectivity and frankness, make a self-examination of their struc-
>   tures, organisations, and methods of work, and the difficulties

that many of them have in their relationships with the national church.

3. We ask for a concrete reaction concerning a model of inter-dependence.

4. We want this consultation to reach the highest levels of 'missionary spheres'. Therefore, we would like the mission representatives present here to indicate how this could best be brought about.

Third World church leaders do not question the *rightness* of missionaries working alongside them, but rather *under whose direction* they should be, and how they should be regarded by the national churches. Theodore Williams, Secretary of the India Missions Association, expressed it thus:

Indian churches do welcome the continued activities of British missionary societies alongside the Indian churches. We do not appreciate these societies *working independently*. I feel that stage is over. I do not believe in the artificial distinction between the church and the Mission. Missionaries should work with the local church.

On another occasion Mr Williams made the point that some missionaries (from the smaller interdenominational societies) are still servants of their missionary societies. 'They are not the servants of the local church, and this is rather unfortunate'.

A Kenyan church leader, John Mbiti, expressed the dilemma thus. 'The Church in Africa has been very missionary-minded but only in terms of receiving missionaries and depending on them'.

One is left to wonder how complete has been the identification between some British missionary societies and the national churches with which they are working, and to what extent missionary societies have been prepared to hand over responsibility; and it would therefore be impertinent of me to make sweeping statements based on insufficient evidence. Patrick Sookhdeo's paper certainly aroused some sharp reactions from delegates at this conference, and a number could with all honesty reply that their societies *were* working towards establishing a true partnership with the Third World churches they had helped to bring to birth in the past.

Two final comments might sum up the direction in which missionary strategists are thinking. Ernest Oliver, Secretary of EMA, said to me on one occasion, 'We've got to let them direct things in their own countries, and we'll throw in our help when they ask for it'. And one resolution of the Lausanne Congress suggested that:

> a *reduction* in foreign missionaries may sometimes be necessary to facilitate the national church's growth in self-reliance and to release resources for unevangelised areas.

Not just another drawing up of a Declaration, one hopes, but an urgent plea for an honest reappraisal of the role of Western missionaries, and for a meaningful dialogue of partnership between missionaries and the new church leaders in the Third World in the eighties.

MISSION IN THE EIGHTIES

If the traditional concept of the mission field has changed to include, not only many miles of rural and sometimes untouched 'jungle' but also rapidly growing and very sophisticated cities, not to mention the Sikhs in the next street, and if missionary societies are also changing their policies and thinking very seriously about the kind of relationship they should be having with the national churches, what about our concept of the traditional missionary? Do we still imagine, or perhaps even entertain a secret hope that, missionaries trained at a missionary college, accept life committment to a society with its Headquarters somewhere in London, and are then posted by a board of godly missionary statesmen (elderly) to a fairly untouched part of the jungle or perhaps to a mission hospital or to a mission school? Do we rather anticipate that their letters home will be interspersed with comments regarding the difficulties they are facing and the hardness of the hearts of the people to whom they have dedicated their lives? And do we expect them to look poor and dowdy, perhaps not able to run a car while on furlough and living in fairly uncongenial surroundings?

Indeed, some of the circumstances mentioned above might still be true of missionaries we know, and still more to the point, might well remind us of the responsibilities that perhaps we have not taken as seriously as we should have done. But although the missionary's sense of divine vocation is still the same, many of the concepts associated with the word 'missionary' have altered. Missionaries today are obeying the same command that the Lord Jesus gave to his disciples, and which compelled Hudson

Taylor and William Carey and a host of others a hundred years ago to leave England for a way of life that was so different from anything that they could begin to understand.

However, missionaries may feel that they cannot today offer their services to a missionary society 'for life' for a number of good reasons. They may feel that they would not want to be separated from their children as they enter their teens; or they may feel that the rapidity of change in many Third World countries demands that a constant flow of new personnel more in tune with the changing scene is better; or they may feel that the total uncertainty surrounding the Third World makes life commitment there impracticable. In fact 19% of British missionaries today are on short term contracts and most missionary societies have a variety of contractual arrangements. BMS for example, accepts youngsters for as short a period as one year, provided that they can raise their own air fare. It also accepts staff for a minimum of two years for a specific project, and again recruits staff for an unlimited period. They do not feel that the former categories are of an inferior calibre to those last-mentioned and accepts that they have skills that may be just right at a particular time, but these skills will be locally available in a few years' time. CMS recruit three categories of missionaries; those who accept a long-term committment (generally for a period of about ten years) and who have a period of two terms' training at the CMS College in Birmingham; the society also recruits volunteers who are prepared to offer a specific skill for a period of one to three years. These normally pay their own fares, but are supported by the institution where they are working. This second group consists largely, but not exclusively, of young people, and some indication of the popularity of the volunteer scheme is that in 1979 78 candidates were accepted from an original list of some 700 enquiries. Finally CMS welcomes members overseas who take up a professional secular post, but wish to enjoy fellowship with the Mission. Members overseas voluntarily pay back part of their Government renumeration into mission funds.

CMS is happy about this 'mix' of missionary categories and in no way regards one group as 'better' or 'more committed' than the others. The General Secretary did point out, however, that the greater turnover demanded a greater volume of applicants and he indicated that recruitment for the long term missionary had fallen off quite critically in recent years.

The Sudan United Mission also have three categories of missionary. They recruit full missionaries, who accept a committment to the Church of Christ in Nigeria. There are also a smaller number (about 10) of *short-term* missionaries within the fellowship who have been recruited for specific skills, usually in teaching and who are most frequently appointed to a specific post, although obviously some flexibility is desirable. Thirdly there are *associate* missionaries (15) who are in fact employed by the Federal Government of Nigeria or a State Government in a professional capacity, but who are recruited by the Church of Christ in Nigeria and share COCIN facilities in terms of education for their children etc. More important, they are welcomed into the mission/church family and enjoy pastoral care. In return they are expected to become members of COCIN, to contribute towards COCIN projects and encourage their home church to be involved in the work of SUM/COCIN. Again associate missionaries have specific contracts for a limited period. Tear Fund operate a STOP programme, which links specific needs to offers of skills for assignments varying in length from three months to four years. Again Tear Fund acts as an agency, receiving requests for Short Term Overseas Personnel from missionary societies, then vetting these projects and matching offers of skills to the requests received. Tear Fund also considers requests from national churches. Once an appointment is made, STOP personnel are seconded to evangelical missionary societies or national churches, but are salaried by Tear Fund, to whom they send regular reports. Basically the STOP programme is concerned with specific skills, usually those concerned with administrations, cottage industry, engineering, health and rural development.

In 1979 a new area of involvement was added to Tear Fund – EPOCH, an acronym for the Evangelical Patnership of Overseas Churches. This programme is concerned with Evangelism and Christian Education, and operates similarly to STOP, in that it recruits for short term commitment and specific evangelistic or pastoral skills. It will continue to act as a sending agency for mission societies, considering their requests and matching these to offers they have received. Tear Fund pointed out, in a recent copy of *Tear Times* that they are increasingly being asked to fill specific vacancies for specific skills. These assignments include: a hydraulic engineer, a weaver, a sewing instructress, a hovercraft instructor, an apiarist, a dentist, a typist and an ecological microbiologist. And, what is more, most of the requests were connected with specific assignments within a clearly defined period of time. One missionary planner reckoned that by the end of this decade more than 80% of missionaries will be on short-term assignments.

So modern missionaries *may* still be recruited by a London missionary society 'for life', and they may indeed be sent to remote areas. But it is just as likely that they will offer their services for a couple of years; it may well be that their home church has, as their missionary project, paid their air fare. It is almost certain that they have specific skills that the Third World needs; they may be young graduates in agriculture, or dentists, or social workers. Alternatively they may have been recruited by the Inter University Council to teach in an African University, by a Government hospital in Bangladesh, or directly by the United Mission to Nepal. They may have been recruited straight from College by VSO. They may be architects, or town planners, going overseas partly because they want to widen their professional experience, but preferring to be identified with a missionary society or national church while overseas, and they have willingly agreed to pay back part of their salary to the church. Indeed they may be an older couple with considerable pastoral experience who feel that, now their children have left home they can offer their services to EPOCH to help with a programme of church education in Nigeria or Brazil.... Or it may be that someone who has recently become ordained feels the call to serve a Church in a large Third World city....

The list of possibilities is endless; the qualifications are a real sense of the divine call to serve overseas, a skill that is needed in the Third World and some experience in that skill, and an ability to *listen* and to adapt. John Aldis succinctly expresses this in the CMS handbook;

> They need to be people of humility and adaptability. People who are prepared to listen and learn; who will share rather than dominate; who are flexible rather than rigid; who can work with others; who can live with frustration and disappointment and who know both how to work and how to rejoice.

And while we are measuring ourselves against these demanding requirements, let us not forget that some Third World churches are doing just the same, as they also send missionaries to other parts of the world. The Church of N. India, for example, has sent one missionary family to E. Africa and another to Fiji, and this example is by no means the only one.

How long before the suggestion made at the 1978 Lambeth Conference is implemented, that Anglican church leaders coming to this country to confer will stay on in order to engage in mission? Evangelists from the Third World have in fact already conducted campaigns here in Britain; Luis Palau from Argentina and Festo Kivengere from Uganda have spoken at public meetings. In 1980 Luis Palau conducted a large-scale evangelistic campaign at the Kelvin Hall, Glasgow. But perhaps we need a concerted mission programme sponsored by a group of Third World churches, who have been burdened for souls in darkest London or Birmingham, and feel the call of God to bring them the Good News!

4

The Church in the Third World

The 'mission scene' has radically changed in the last twenty-five years, and will go on changing in the next twenty-five; this point was firmly established in the previous chapter. Although no doubt some missionary societies have so far succeeded in putting their heads down and ignoring the wind of change, and certainly some missionaries have found the gale too much for them, the majority of societies in this country have been aware of the need to establish new attitudes and relationships between themselves and the new national churches they have helped to bring into being. As a general rule they are sensitive to the *right* of national churches to determine the deployment of overseas workers who come to work alongside them. But what of the national churches? What particular problems and opportunities are they facing in the '80s?

THE GROWTH OF THE CHURCH IN THE THIRD WORLD

In the first place, the churches in the Third World *are growing rapidly*. Whereas in Chapter 1, we were reminded that numerically the Church in Britain is declining, the opposite is true in the Third World. There are some 135 million Christians in Africa today, 33% of the total population, and on the basis of a survey carried out by Dr Barrett, compiler of the *World Christian Handbook*, this figure is expected to reach 300 million by 2000AD. One estimate reckons that African Christians are increasing at four times the rate of the general population increase. The same exciting story is true in S. America. In 1970 there were 19,000,000 Protestant Christians in Latin America, and the rate of church growth each year is 10%, in comparison with an overall population growth of 3%. In fact the church in S. America is the fastest growing church in the world. In Asia there are approximately 70 million Christians, and the rate of church growth is three times the rate of the overall population increase.

But Third World church growthis not merely to be measured in terms of numbers. SU International reports an increase of 5% in the worldwide circulation of Bible reading notes and cards in the years 1976-78, and the respective increase for Africa is no less than 26%. IFES (International Fellowship of Evangelical Students) reports that student interest in the Christian faith in Third World Universities and High Schools is unparalleled, as thinking young people long for a way of life that can transform their lives and many find this, not in the writings of Karl Marx or Jean Paul Sartre or Fritz Fanon, but in a personal committment to Christ. And at a time when many British missionary societies report that they are just holding their own financially, and when missionary recruitment is generally low and societies are having to advertise to attract recruits, Third World churches have in the last ten years sent 3,000 missionaries to other parts of the Third World, in many cases to countries with a cultural and language background quite different from their own. One writer ventured the hope that by 2000 AD Asia will have sent out 10,000 missionaries to other parts of the world. It may not be totally without significance that the Evangelical Alliance survey on initiatives in evangelism, (1979) showed that 13.1% of those who responded to the survey indicated that they favoured the Argentinian evangelist Luis Palau as the chosen evangelist to visit Britain in the '80s. (In the same survey, 52.5% believed that, if there is to be a national outreach Billy Graham should be invited to lead it.) *Crusade* (June 1979) carried a major article describing an evangelistic campaign in Scotland led by Luis Palau and offered the sub-heading – 'Will Billy Graham's mantle fall on the shoulders of Luis Palau?'

Third World churches are growing, therefore, not simply in terms of mere numbers, but of much greater significance, they are alive and aware, making a tremendous impact upon the societies in which they are placed. They are well on the way towards autonomy, and are discovering a new and very constructive relationship with their former spiritual leaders the missionaries.

CHANGING PATTERNS OF WORSHIP

They are also seeking to establish their own identity in terms of worship and expression. Readers may be familiar with David Fanshawe's *African Sanctus* or the *Lubba Mass* or other musical expressions from Africa that have found their way to Britain. But these full-blooded African expressions of worship are the exception rather than the rule; English (or American) hymns and patterns of worship are still far more common. I can well remember singing choruses from 'CSSM 1 and 2' at an SU camp in Africa, long after British congregations had relegated these to the old-fashioned category.

I was encouraged to learn from Theo Dankwa, who was a travelling secretary with The International Fellowship of Evangelical Students in Ghana before coming to London Bible College to read for a BA in Theology, that school and college groups are beginning to feel liberated from Western associations in music; but the African students I met at LBC felt that there was a danger of a new cult emerging – that of singing choruses without much biblical content. Perhaps this trend is not limited to Africa!

National churches in the Third World have still to work out their own idiom, in terms of music and liturgy, as well as in church government. This process will take time and may result in an interim period of 'liturgical syncretism' – hymns Ancient and Modern interspersed with Kumbiyaa! One of the difficulties to be overcome is the extent to which Western patterns of worship and liturgy have become part of the cultural package and environment of those Christians who have been educated overseas, and then return to their home countries to take up executive positions and worship in 'fashionable' churches in the cities. Go to most of the popular city churches in a large Third World city and you will find a pattern of worship that is more English than the English! You would be much more likely to find a more spontaneous expression of local worship in the village churches or in a down-town fellowship.

There is another, more significant, reason why those in church leadership are nervous of encouraging Christians to express themselves too completely in the local idiom. The pioneer missionaries were so stern in their denunciation of 'heathen practices', (by which they meant not just ancestor worship and juju, but also African music and rhythm), that their successors today, the indigenous church leaders, are afraid that pagan elements might slip in again if the local idiom is given too much rein. One Nigerian church leader spoke of the quest for cultural authenticity as questionable and leading to idolatry. The whole matter of tribal dancing is one example of this dilemma. Undoubtedly some African dancing – and indeed British dancing too – has strong sexual overtones, but it would be totally wrong to write it off as completely evil. On the contrary, rhythm and physical movement is deeply imbued in the African way of life and expression. Surely it should not be excluded from Christian worship! In any case, rhythm and dance are increasingly used in worship today in Western churches also.

Although problems like the one mentioned above might seem a little remote to Christians in the West, they are very real in parts of the Third World where the church is still defining its boundaries in respect of indigenous cultural practices.

On a more positive note, evangelicals throughout Africa have cooperated to open a new graduate school of theology in Nairobi, to train church and Bible college leaders 'sensitive to the needs, issues and cultures of a rapidly changing continent' – clearly a move in the right direction!

The Church in the Third World, then, is seeking to find forms of worship and expression that are biblical, local and spontaneous. Some are also beginning to experiment with new forms of church structures. Perhaps British church systems and liturgical forms have remained more deeply imbued in Africa than in other Third World churches, but the stamp of missionary habits and structures can still be clearly recognised in most countries in Africa. What tends to happen is that the independent church structures that have been established once the actual control has passed from missionary hands are identical to those that were built up by the missionaries fifty years ago, but without the Europeans at the top. They are simply not thought out through African minds – organisational change tends to come later.

The African scene has been dominated by British patterns; in Malysia the predominant influence has been American. American church structures and patterns of worship remain, and are in some cases more deeply embedded in the local church than the British patterns in Africa. Some missionary societies were careful when first establishing their work in a new country to demarcate certain areas as within their proper 'spheres of influence', so that unnecessary duplication did not occur. In Zaïre, for example, the major European societies did work out a strategy along these lines. In other cases, notably where different missionary societies with quite divergent theological emphases were involved, this did not happen, and until recently this led to some denominational overlap, and in some cases, competition. Thus any sizeable town in Ghana, for example, would have an Anglican Church, placed under the direction of a diocese complete with bishop, diocesan council and offices; a Methodist Church within a circuit complete with circuit stewards; a Presbyterian Church (on the Swiss model); and a Catholic Church – as well as a Seventh Day Adventist Church, an Assemblies of God Church, and in some cases also a Baptist Church, or a Salvation Army Citadel. Bear in mind that many of these denominational groups also superintend schools, and one can appreciate the complexity of the denominational scene in Ghana until recently.

In some countries this multiplicity of denominational groups is beginning to change, however. The three major denominational groups in Ghana, for example (the Anglican Church, Methodist Church of Ghana and the Evangelical Presbyterians) have recently amalgamated. One hopes that the details of this amalgamation will be worked out without friction, and that the resulting unified church structure will be effective, and make for the greater witness of Jesus Christ in that country.

A proliferation of denominational groups in Third World churches might be perfectly acceptable in some situations, but it might well be that it acts as a hindrance to the Gospel in others. The important issue is for each national church to come to its own decision as to the structure it finds most suitable, and to change the existing former colonial pattern if it deems fit.

In some countries, Governments have insisted on a programme of Church amalgamation. In Zaïre, for example, only three churches are recognised; the Protestant Church; the Roman Catholic Church; and the Kimbanguist Church. Mission fits into this pattern; thus, for example, the BMS identify with the Baptist Community of the River Zaïre. Again, there are two large church groups in India – the United Church of North India and the Church of South India. These are not exclusive groups, however, and some denominational groups have not joined either of these groups.

One very interesting and remarkably successful experiment in mission cooperation has been the United Mission to Nepal. For many years, European missionary enterprise, including direct proselytisation and therefore any programme of church planting, has been forbidden by Government decree in Nepal, but in 1954 the Government of Nepal gave permission for missionary societies to commence a medical programme in Tansen and the

Khatmandu valley. A group of eight missionary societies, under the guidance of Ernest Oliver, a missionary with many years' experience in North India, formed themselves into the *United Christian Mission to Nepal* (later changed to the United Mission to Nepal). The UMN received a specific mandate from the Government of Nepal to engage in 'project work', but they may not 'propagate Christianity, Islam, or any other faith so as to disrupt the traditional religion of the Hindu community within Nepal, or convert any adherent of the Hindu religion into these faiths'. Today their projects include a medical programme, with responsibility for three hospitals and a number of community health schemes; an educational programme, which includes seconded teachers to secondary schools and a University; a Technical Institute and a number of experts seconded to technical development schemes, and a small community development programme. The UMN is a single organisation, drawing its members from 28 missionary societies which represent a dozen leading denominational societies and as many interdenominational societies drawn from 15 countries, including Europe, North America and Australasia. Although each member missionary society continues to support its own missionaries financially and to look after their children's education etc., these missionaries become the servants of the UMN while in Nepal. Thus they can devote their energies singlemindedly to the project to which they are seconded, and are not concerned to extend the influence, or increase the number of churches within the control of the missionary societies that originally recruited them. For many, this freedom has become a 'blessed liberty', and has set them free to serve the Lord in the manner best suited to the project to which they have been assigned. Individual missionary society control is limited to membership of the Board of Directors which meets regularly in Khatmandu.

Personnel working within the UMN have a definite mandate from the Government of Nepal to train Nepalese workers to take over the posts of foreign workers as soon as possible. The Mission has to inform the Government of its progress and plans, and submit annual reports to the appropriate departments. But the UMN is growing rapidly; in 1954 there were 7 missionaries within the fellowship; in 1978 there were 237. The Christian community in Nepal is also growing; the Nepal Christian Fellowship, an informal association linking small and often geographically isolated fellowships together, is growing rapidly, and converts are being added daily. Missionaries (under the auspices of UMN or the smaller International Nepal Fellowship) support the Nepal Christian Fellowship in a variety of ways, offering their advice and help in a supportive role.

Thus the Church in Nepal has avoided the difficulties that have been caused by too much fragmentation, as has happened in many Third World countries, and missionaries have used their skills in helping the overall programme of national development.

It may be that the process of meaningful church unity will begin in the Third World, therefore, and that the British based multiplicity of missionary societies will wither away because of the changed situation 'on the field'. Missionary societies will have to decide whether to join the new united national churches or to stand aloof from them. Obviously their decision will be influenced to some extent by the theological flavour of the particular national church, but one would hope for the sake of the national Christians, that missionary societies will do everything possible to identify with the new national structures.

One other development in terms of Third World church structure has been the emergence of a *further* church unit in a number of Third World countries – formed and dominated by an individual. Reference has already been made to the Kimbanguist Church in Zaïre. This church was founded by Simon Kimbangu, a man with tremendous charismatic appeal, and although he was for some years imprisoned by the Belgians for fear of the possible political consequences of his following, a church has mushroomed around him. The Kimbanguist Church has developed a style distinctly African, and is strong in terms of enthusiasm and local colour, but less secure in its theology, combining certain elements of pre-Christian African thought and tradition with Christian theology. And Kimbanguism, with its obvious appeal, has numerous counterparts in other parts of Africa. Some are totally acceptable in terms of a biblical theology, others far less so. The Lumpa sect in Zambia, for example, was definitely not totally biblical in its theology.

Another more positive movement in many Third World countries (again notably in Africa and Singapore) is the growth of charismatic Churches. These groups are characterised by phenomena similar to those in similar groups in this country – a greater informality and involvement in worship, speaking in tongues, the giving of prophecies and healing meetings. A potential area of danger in some Third World charismatic groups, however, is the emergence of very powerful individual charismatic leaders. Some of these assume biblical titles, like the Apostle Barnabas in Ghana. Although these charismatic leaders may indeed be men of God and pastors of their people, others may be false shepherds, out to exploit their position for their own ends. *The Believer*, a weekly newspaper published in Ghana, carried a leading article in an edition (published in August 1979) headed 'Prophetess deceives poor soul', and told the sad story of a young man who went to the Prophetess of the Jerusalem Healing Church to seek help with his personal problems. He was promised that all his problems would be solved if he agreed to fast for seventeen days. He was then told to undergo certain rites at the sea shore, and asked to pay a considerable sum of money. But the young man found that he had been misled and his money wasted. Such stories are sadly only too common as churches of this kind fall under the influence of less principled or misguided leaders.

The Church of Christ, therefore, has on the one hand to defend the Faith from those elements that are clearly unbiblical, be on guard against those elements that are of uncertain theological pedigree and on the other to develop a style and a liturgy, as well as a structure, that is truly indigenous. And the missionary must stand back and offer advice only when asked – no easy task!

THE CHURCH AND OTHER IDEOLOGIES

But the Church in the Third World is not growing in an ideological vacuum. Recent events in Iran have again brought home to us the tremendous power of Islam in the Middle East. But there are also over 150 million Muslims in Africa today out of a total population of 400 million (and sizeable Muslim communities exist in West, Central and East Africa as well as in North Africa, where the population is nearly totally Muslim). About 100 million live in Indonesia and Malaysia. Pakistan and Bangladesh are both Muslim States, although the Christian church is given considerable freedom and at present missionaries may preach openly. On the other hand, the situation for Christians in Afghanistan and Iran is very much more difficult. Islam like Christianity is credal and makes specific demands upon its followers. They have an obligation to come to the aid of fellow-Muslims in need (and this fellowship of Muslims overcomes all colour differences), a further obligation to support a Muslim war, or jihad, considerable financial demands, and a total abstinence from alcohol – hence the strict laws passed in Muslim countries against brewing alcohol and the fierce punishments for those who are caught trading liquor. Despite this demanding legal aspect of Muslim belief, overall the Muslim faith has an excellent ethical content and does expect high standards from its adherents. It is, of course, fiercely monotheistic and a Muslim finds tremendous difficulty in understanding the Christian doctrine of the Trinity. We would do well to remember that Islam, unlike much middle-class Western Christianity, is *not* a private affair. To many practising Muslims, religion, culture and a total life-style are synonymous and therefore it is quite in order for Iran and Pakistan to introduce strict laws against theft, alcohol and sexual offences. If these are crimes against Allah, then they are crimes against the State, and the State has every right to punish those who defy the rules of Allah. Thus to state that Pakistan and Bangladesh are Muslim countries has much more significance than to affirm, for example, that Britain is a Christian country.

Perhaps it is because of the all-embracing nature of Islam that it makes its strongest appeal to the traditionalist elements in a Third World society; it favours the status quo and is nervous of the disruptive influences of the West. It can be said to favour the male sex, in that a Muslim man may have more than one wife and the man is certainly regarded as the stronger partner in the relationship. On the other hand, Islam is less popular in the large towns, where the lure of Western technology and materialism is greater and is seen to erode the values of Islam.

Christian missionaries have hitherto regarded Islam as totally antipathetic to Christianity and have confronted Muslims 'head on'. But this aggressive policy is changing, as Christians and Muslims begin to appreciate a certain measure of common ground. This is certainly not the case however at present in the Middle East, where there is clearly a growth of militant Islam. This will undoubtedly have repercussions on the Christian churches there, as well as in North Africa and elsewhere and the situation will not be made easier in that Islam may major in its condemnation of the corrupt materialism of the West and point to the damaging cultural effects of Western colonialism/capitalism in its efforts to proselytise, or to win back those who have forsaken the Muslim faith.

Perhaps also we should not forget that one estimate reckons

the number of Muslims in Britain to be nearly half a million; and there are at least 300 mosques in this country!

Islam is not the only religion that the Christian churches in the Third World will have to face; Marxism, although perhaps not generally classified as a religious faith, has had considerable appeal to very many in the Third World. The reasons for its appeal are not hard to discover. It can effectively, and to some extent with justification, castigate the evils of imperialism, and although not all its adherents necessarily understand the doctrinaire arguments of Marx and Lenin, or even Fanon or Castro, regarding the causes and effects of imperialism, they are content to associate with a political ideology that can produce quite convincing arguments emphasising the ways in which the Western powers have exploited them in the past. Further, Marxism offers a very convincing rationale of economic inequality, and can also guarantee that a true Marxist-type society will change that inequitable system.

Marxism, or more properly Communism, *has* changed societies. It has transformed Russia from a backward feudal state to one of the most advanced technological societies in the world. Likewise it has transformed China from a society that virtually stood still for three hundred years to one of the new Superpowers, and one that neither the USSR nor the USA would wish to engage in military conflict. And Communism, or local variants of Communist philosophy, has had tremendous effects in some areas in the Third World. But doctrinaire Marxism, in the nature of its ideology, must be opposed to some of the basic doctrines of Christianity, and the adherents of liberation theology have also needed to come to this conclusion. This is because for a Communist the basic doctrines of the nature of man and of the root causes of wrong in human society are diametrically opposed to the Christian view of a fallen man resulting in a fallen society, and where a state or a society has adopted Marxist philosophy, the national church has inevitably come under fire.

This is not to say, however, that certain aspects of Communism may not in fact be appropriate in a Third World society today, because manifestly they are. Julius Nyerere, President of Tanzania, is himself a committed Catholic, an obvious God fearer, and he is also deeply in favour of certain aspects of the Chinese way of life. He has said so publicly, and encouraged the Tanzanian people to adopt these. So it is quite wrong of certain of our American or British brethren to equate Communism in every aspect with the devil. I quote in this context from a sermon preached by Rev Brian Williams, self-styled evangelist, at Trinity Methodist Church, Salisbury, Rhodesia in 1976;

> There are two observations I would make. Firstly, there is a much greter likelihood of Britain turning Communist before ever Rhodesia does. Secondly, the Scripture says, 'God is not mocked; for whatever a man soweth, that shall he also reap.' If we sow good we shall reap good, if we sow evil we shall reap evil, and this is true not only of individuals but also of nations. Ever since the British Government decided that it would smash the Rhodesian economy by the imposition of sanctions, it is not the Rhodesian economy that has been smashed but the British economy, so that whereas there were two Rhodesian dollars to the British pound when we were here ten years ago, our British pound is now worth only 95 cents.
>   I want you to notice that the Scripture says there cometh a great multitude against thee. I do not need to enlarge upon this fact tonight that Rhodesia stands against the whole world might of the Communist empire, against the whole of world opinions. Rhodesia stands tonight as almost the last bastion of Christian civilisation, and one hesitates to think what might happen if Rhodesia and South Africa should fall to the Communist plague.

Although this is an extreme view, I would hazard a guess that there is a Christian lobby that regards any manifestation of Communism in the Third World as totally evil.

We would do well to be clear that, while on the one hand Marxism as a philosophy originally propounded by Karl Marx and subsequent Marxist political thinkers is unbiblical and opposed to the way of life expounded by Jesus, on the other hand certain aspects of communism (with a small 'c') and certain political experiments now being attempted in the Third World might well be closer to the pattern and behaviour of the early church than we would perhaps readily wish to recognise. And we might well pause to consider whether a truly Christian society in the late twentieth century would not do well to adopt certain aspects of communism, in the sense that it is willing to undertake a much more radical policy of sharing material possessions (Acts 4:32-7)!

Christian church leaders in a number of Third World states are faced with the sensitive problem of knowing how to relate to a political regime that is at least in part Marxist. The Christian communities in Zanzibar and in Cuba are two cases in point. Another area of extreme difficulty arises when a regime becomes patently evil, or so riddled with corruption that honest business transactions become virtually impossible. In the search for a political and economic philosophy suitable to the local situation power has on occasions fallen into unscrupulous hands. Man is no less in a state of fallen humanity in the Third World than in the West! Alternatively it may be that a group of politicians who have led the people to independence have built up so much charisma that power goes to their heads. Both dangers can be illustrated in the recent Third World scene. President Bhutto's regime in Pakistan became increasingly corrupt until it was terminated.

Kwame Nkrumah of Ghana was ousted in 1965 as a mad megalomaniac. Nkrumah should rather be remembered as the greatest pioneer in political nationalism in Africa in the '40s and '50s, because not only did he bring Ghana to birth in 1957, but he also made Accra the venue for a number of significant Pan-African conferences; undoubtedly the city became a seminary for Independence plans that were later to come into operation elsewhere. Yet power went to Nkrumah's head, and in fact some of those who took part in the military exercise that overthrew him were known to be Christian men. One of the problems the Ghanaian Church had to face in the early '60s was Nkrumahism – a cult little short of deification of the man. Should the Church succumb to the adulation of Nkrumah that was generally practised then? Or should they oppose it, and in the final analysis take an active part in his overthrow? This kind of dilemma has been repeated in a number of African States, the most recent being the atrocious regime of President Amin in Uganda. Archbishop Luwum was not the only Christian to suffer a martyr's death in Uganda in the late '70s; the evidence is rather that there was a systematic persecution of Christian leaders. Christians have had to contend with violence and oppression in Ethiopia, Angola and elsewhere.

The Church in Pakistan, Bangladesh and Afghanistan has had to contend with another problem vis-a-vis its relationship with the State. These countries are Muslim States, and although other religious beliefs are tolerated, preaching the Gospel is not generally allowed. In any case the ethos of the State is specifically Muslim. Once again the Church has had to grapple with the difficulty of interpreting Romans 13:1–2, and it is important that the kind of stand that they do make is their own, and not seen as a pale mirror of European thinking. There have been occasions when the presence of the missionary has been something of an embarrassment, because he has been seen by the national politicians not only as a representative of the colonial stock, but also as holding views unsympathetic to the political experiment that is being attempted. Moreover he may even have been heard to denounce the regime under which he is living as Marxist or tyrannical – neither of which accusation may be true. Thus there are times when Third World Church leaders must be seen to be making their own decisions with regard to their relationship with the secular power, and the decisions they finally make may not always be those of which their fellow missionaries and former spiritual leaders would have approved. It is not always easy for the missionary to stand back and allow Church leaders, some of whom may be his personal friends, to grapple with these very difficult situations without feeling that he ought to advise, but this may indeed be one very necessary lesson missionaries in the '80s have to learn.

LIBERATION THEOLOGY

Reference has already been made to some Evangelicals' reluctance to get deeply involved in matters of social concern, and to Tear Fund's role in providing an avenue through which Evangelicals can channel their expressions of care for those in material need. *Liberation theology* represents a Third World response to this need to produce a theological comment on the problems of inequality in the contemporary world. The movement can be said to have originated with a book written by Richard Shaull, a missionary in Columbia – *Encounter with Revolution*, and subsequently with a discussion group within the World Council of Churches – *Church and Society*. This action group has undoubtedly had a considerable influence on the WCC's thinking, and as the WCC's assembly at Nairobi in 1976 indicated, Church leaders are very sensitive to the implications *for the Church* of the widening gap between rich and poor countries, and the extent to which some Western countries' economic structures are seen to perpetuate that gap. The same issue exercised the Roman Catholic Churches, and in 1968 the Latin American episcopate took a very radical stance on issues of social justice and political and economical oppression. They perceived the under-developed nations as abjectly dependent on the decisions of those who control the means of production. Third World countries must 'liberate' themselves from such subjugation.

Thus Liberation Theology was born. 'Liberation Theology attempts to elaborate the whole content of Christianity, beginning from the demands of social liberation' – *Theology out of Captivity*—Boff 1976. It has been deeply influenced by the present unequal society in South America, where wholesale urban unemployment and rural stagnation live side by side with affluence, and it puts much of the blame for this state of affairs upon North American influences, both political and theological. It argues that the Marxist analysis of the present evils of society – the ownership of the means of production by the few capitalist magnates – and the need to overthrow this decadent society by some form of class struggle has something to commend it. Liberation theologians argue (with justification) that Jesus preached liberation to the poor, and that this message has a direct relevance to the poor in South America in the 1980s. Liberation Theology has undoubtedly had a startling effect on Third World churches, particularly those in South America. Yet it cannot be the full Gospel; for Marxism neither admits *all men's* need for salvation at the Cross of Christ, regardless of their social or economic class, nor does it admit the transforming power of Christ to enable men to share their possessions out of *love* for one another, rather than through any State organised coercion. And Liberation Theology has found it impossible to reconcile the Marxist analysis of the ills of human society and the teaching of Jesus Christ. Liberation Theology as a system is on the decline in the '80s, but again Third World leaders in the church have had to work out their own response to this new and very appealing theology that had something very specific to say about the local situation. As we have already seen, missionaries have again had to come to grips with the *physical* and *material* needs of men and women in the Third World, and not see themselves merely as preachers of the Gospel in a restricted sense. Rather they have had again to remind themselves that Jesus fed the multitudes and healed the sick as well as preaching the Gospel to them; and they have considered afresh the exhortations of James 2. They do indeed meet brethren and sisters who need clothes and don't have enough to eat, and it is quite wrong merely to tell them 'to keep warm and eat well'. The missionary may well have to set to and help provide these poor brethren and sisters with food and shelter!

NEW STRUCTURES FOR NEW CHURCHES

The Third World church in the '80s, then, faces tremendous difficulties. It is seeking to discover its own identity in terms of worship and structure, and this will mean on the one hand avoiding the tacit acceptance of British traditions without critical consideration, but on the other not allowing pagan elements to creep in under the guise of local expression. The Church in many parts of the Third World is also seeking to come to terms with political patterns that are new and untried, in some cases accepting systems of which the missionaries may disapprove, but are still appropriate in the particular national context in which they are being tried. On the other hand, there have been – and will continue to be – occasions when a Government's activities are denounced by the national church, and Christians will need spiritual discernment to know when this situation has been reached, and courage to make a stand. The Church in the Third World is also seeking to clarify its thinking regarding an unequal social and economic world. In all these extremely complex decision-making situations, it has to defend the whole Gospel of Christ. Surely these are no easy tasks for it to tackle! How much Christians need spiritual discernment (Colossians 1:9) to help them in their task!

One final difficulty which is to some extent shared by churches in the West – galloping inflation. This is common to nearly all the Third World in the '80s, and in some countries has reached alarming proportions. It affects the Church in a number of ways. In some countries it makes foreign exchange transactions exceedingly difficult; in Ghana, for example, the Africa Christian Press cannot buy books printed in England, and in many African countries mission hospitals find that they cannot purchase the drugs and equipment they need from abroad.It means that accommodation for pastors is prohibitively expensive in the cities, and also exacerbates the gulf between the poorer congregations in the rural areas and their richer brethren in the towns. This last problem can create real difficulties, because most Third World societies have a much greater care for their extended family than we do in the West, and it is only too easy for the fortunate member who manages to get a job in the town to forget his poorer relations in the villages – in fact, sometimes he has to forget them because otherwise they would drain him of his resources! Perhaps it is in this context that the appeal of Liberation Theology may be more fully appreciated; the large and perhaps 'fashionable' churches that exist in many of the larger towns of the Third World and the emergence of a privileged few church leaders or unattached evangelists jet-setting to various conferences across the world are seen by radical theologians as being little more than copies of a decadent capitalist West, and should have no place in a Christian expression that sees gross inequality in living standards as theologically wrong.

A further difficulty that stems from galloping inflation is that of the consequent corruption. Reference has already been made to this problem, and the vexed question the church has to face is to know when to make a public stand against it. Should a minister of a Church in a large African or Indian city be prepared to rebuke a Cabinet Minister who is a member of his congregation and who is known to be involved in corrupt dealings in Parliament, or a business man who has succumbed to the enormous temptation to secure a contract by paying the required 'dash'? These are difficult questions to answer, and they can only be answered by the Christians who are actually living in these situations, guided by their own elders and pastors.

But the church in the Third World is growing by leaps and bounds, and there is every indication that men and women are increasingly turning to the Gospel of Christ as the Way of Life that most completely satisfies their needs. Political independence has not brought the Utopia that some politicians promised – in fact Independence has brought a cluster of new problems. And human greed and jealously remain. The Church of Christ promises a new and better way.

I invited respresentatives of a number of Third World churches to offer a contribution describing some developments within their own churches. A couple are summarised below.

India
The first, written by Theodore Williams, Secretary of the Indian Mission Association, offers a timely reminder that not all missionary enterprise has come from Europe or North America. The Mar Thoma Syrian Church in Kerala organised its own Evangelistic Association in 1888, and fifteen years later the Indian Missionary Society was formed, sending missionaries to work among people of other languages and cultures in the sub-continent. Other denominational churches have also sent missionaries – from the Church of North India to East Africa and Fiji, and the

Naga Baptist Churches support missionaries in the North East region, for example. The National Missionary Society and the Indian Evangelical Mission (both nationwide bodies) have workers in Nepal and Papua New Guinea. Theodore Williams writes describing the financial support of Indian missionaries.

> Personalised support is common. A prayer band or a local church or sometimes even a family takes care of the support of a missionary family. A local church may sometimes support missionaries from two or three missions. Missionaries are not expected to raise their own support. Sometimes, instead of money, gifts in kind are given. In one place, every time the housewife cooks a meal of rice, she puts aside a handful of rice as a missionary offering. In another place a hen is set apart for missions so that its eggs are sold and the money used for missionary support. A large percentage of the support comes from the urban churches.

Several Indian missions have their own Bible schools to train their workers, and in 1976 the Indian Missionary Training Institute was established, and it is hoped that eventually all Indian missionaries will use this Institute. As a further step in cooperation, an association of Indian missions was formed in 1977 to link together the missionary societies, all of them formed and organised on Indian soil, into a meaningful partnership.

Central Africa

John Howell, Deputy Executive Officer of the Nairobi-based Lausanne Committee for World Evangelisation, described another development in the African church; inter-church co-operation across a continent where *physical* communication from one country to another can be exceedingly difficult, let alone *spiritual* communication. Colonial history has made sure that communications between African and European capitals are easy, but it is much more difficult to travel from (e.g.) Accra to Salisbury or Kinshasha than from these capitals to Europe! But Christians representing different cultural backgrounds are getting together, both to worship and share their experiences of the Lord and also to plan for more effective witness in the Continent in the '80s. John Howell writes:

> The Association of Evangelicals of Africa and Madagascar aims to draw evangelicals together to stand for the Lord Jesus Christ and the truth of his Word. It aims to provide spiritual fellowship as a means of

united actions among Christians of like faith; to manifest before the world true Biblical unity; to promote evangelism and Church growth and to alert Christians to the theological trends that undermine the Scriptural foundation of the Gospel.

In 1973 the AEAM established two permanent commissions.

1. The Theological Commission, which includes a new Graduate School of Theology, recently opened in Nairobi. In a brochure outlining the aims and objectives of this new school, Sam Odunaike, President of AEAM, wrote:

Nor does the answer lie in sending Africans to Western countries for postgraduate training. This course of action will be necessary for some years to come, but it is increasingly suspect by African communities who see the church yielding to excessive Western influence. We are grateful for this necessary interim help, but the time is overdue to replace it with our own African Answer.

2. The Christian Education Commission.
This commission helps the churches in Africa strengthen their teaching ministries by acting as a resource bank for activities within the sphere of Christian education across Africa. It encourages Christian education leadership conferences and training programmes and conducts research projects to promote more effective Christian education in Africa in the future.

Another interesting example of inter-church cooperation is the Church of Christ in Zaïre, which includes 53 member communities (formerly denominations) and seeks to encourage all Zaïrean Christians to take an active part in witnessing for Christ.

A further expression of cooperation was the Pan African Christian Leadership Assembly (PACLA), born as a result of the Lausanne Congress on World Evangelisation. PACLA exists basically to widen the potential of leadership quality throughout Africa, and seeks to tackle those forces that obstruct Christian witness, such as racialism, poverty, urbanization and syncretism. Although PACLA was seen by some as tending to duplicate the work and objectives of other structures it has come into being and, among other tasks, has published a number of booklets relating to Christianity in Africa.

Thus Third World churches in India and Africa and indeed in South America, the Caribbean and South East Asia, are beginning to explore ways in which they can purposefully cooperate, with a view to spreading the Gospel more effectively. Communication problems *are* enormous. As John Howell suggests in his paper, it might well take much longer for a consignment of books to travel from Lagos to Nairobi than for the same consignment to travel from Lagos to London. And these vast distances make communication of ideas and of fellowship difficult. But ideas are circulating, as Christians in one Third World country want to share their experiences of the Lord and also discuss ways in which they are tackling the issues of the day with Christians in another country – or even another continent. Sometimes, but not always, missionaries are involved in the bridge-building process. John Howell, an Australian, whose article is quoted above, is the assistant to Gottfried Osei-Mensah, a Ghanaian, who is Executive Secretary of the Lausanne Committee for World Evangelization with offices in Nairobi! And the motto of this group is 'Let the Earth hear His voice'!

A hundred and twenty-five years ago, David Livingstone urged the undergraduates of Cambridge to take the Gospel to Africa while there was still time. Half a century later C. T. Studd urged another generation of undergraduates to evangelise the world in his generation. Neither of these great pioneers in mission evangelism could have conceived of the vitality, spiritual maturity and rapid growth of the churches they helped to found. For in the Third World, if not here in Great Britain, the Church of Jesus Christ is growing 'like a mighty army', and if C. T. Studd's vision is to be fulfilled in this generation, its execution will be done as much by Christian preachers and evangelists, teachers and communicators from India and Africa, Malaysia and 'the uttermost parts of the earth', as by Western based missionaries. We can only stop reading for a moment and give praise to God for the vision that was given to David Livingstone, to Henry Martyn, to William Carey, to C. T. Studd, to Len Moules . . . and rejoice that this same vision is now being pursued by Luis Palau, by Gottfried Osei-Mensah, by Festo Kivengere and by many other Christian leaders in the Third World, many of whom have indeed addressed Christian gatherings in this country.

One word in conclusion. This chapter, and to a lesser extent the two previous chapters, have taken some quite hard knocks at the West and its impact upon the Third World in the last hundred years – and rightly so. Victorian imperialists and their descendants have been guilty of despising cultures foreign to them and in many cases causing them to become stunted in their growth. Many men and women have been culturally wounded and their sensitivities trampled on. European business men, and indirectly their shareholders, have exploited the resources of the Third World for their own advantages. But resentment towards the

West should find no place in the Church of Christ. Church leaders may be critical of certain aspects of the West, as the following comment from Zaïrean evangelist Mavumilusa Makanzu illustrates:

> Where the West is retreating spiritually, Africa is advancing. The African has decided to love the Bible with all his heart. Keep your novels and your horoscopes and sell us Bibles. We prefer to die rather than end up candidates for atheism. Not the horrors of modern war, not the sufferings of famine, nor dollars, nor anything else will turn us into atheists. We love the Bible more than our earthly lives. It is not only a book of God, but a letter written by God to the African soul.

But the key point to note is that missionaries and national Christian leaders are working together for the good of the church. Leadership roles have on a number of occasions been reversed and new kinds of relationships established, but the two orders share a unity in Christ that allows for no grudges or paying back old scores. *And this really does happen.* The redemptive power of Christ has in many cases healed the slights that may have occurred in the past and made possible a new and mature oneness, as both missionaries and national Christians together acknowledge the Lordship of Christ and share in this very exciting chapter in Church development.

5

The Third World and the Church in Britain

The material offered so far in this book demands a response. Indeed, some of the statistical and factual information about the poverty existing in parts of the Third World will have caused us deep disquiet. Even more so, perhaps, when we bear in mind the many faces of poverty – for the word covers not only a basic lack of food and shelter, but equally inadequate medical facilities and educational opportunities, especially in rural areas. We simply cannot close our minds to some of the disturbing facts concerning the needs of the Third World if we are to accept and act upon the consistent and often repeated biblical teaching about sharing and caring for those less fortunate than ourselves. The Lord's instructions to care for those who are hungry...or thirsty...or naked as though we were caring for him (Matt. 25:37–39) may take on a new significance for us, having become aware of the poverty in which some of our brothers and sisters in Christ are having to live today.

Yet the 'message' of this book is *not* just a plea for more help for an impoverished Third World. Indeed, if this is the strongest signal that the reader has so far picked up, then the book has miscarried. First and foremost, it has been written to inform and to help people gain a new perspective on the contemporary Third World. Too many Christians have not thought beyond the now mercifully outmoded Oxfam image of the Third World and equate that part of the world with a syndrome of poverty: no attempt to control the population explosion, absolutely no motivation on the part of the local population to improve their standard of living, but rather an unthinking dependence upon foreign aid in one form or another. *But the Third World is not like that*. Perhaps the most urgent priority for the intelligent Christian today is to refocus his image of the Third World, to increase his depth of vision, and if necessary to fit an entirely new lens in order to correct the blurred images that may have been formerly passed on from some missionary societies and aid agencies. His new field of vision will include the rapidly-growing cosmopolitan cities of the Third World, with their attendant social problems, as extremes of wealth and poverty jostle in ever closer proximity, yet with every evidence that the only form of communication between the two is based upon fear. Readers will have noticed that the Pan-African Christian Leaders' Association regarded *urbanisation* as one of the forces that obstruct Christian witness (page 102), and included this area of social change in the same bracket as racialism and poverty.

A new view of Third World cities will include a growing tourist industry, with all its attendant evils, as well as obvious advantages. For tourism introduces a new, and often an alien, materialism and hedonism into societies that a couple of generations ago were basically peasant economies. On the other hand, tourism provides employment for some who would otherwise have no opportunity to earn a regular wage. It also brings much-needed sterling or dollars to the country concerned. On balance, tourism has harmed Jamaican society but has stimulated certain areas of the economy in East Africa.

The observer will have to catch in his vision not only the enormous problems of unemployment in the Third World but also the interaction between employment and wage patterns, and the new markets created by the demands of the West. He will have to work out for himself the moral dilemma caused by multinational companies anxious to increase their profits from Third World markets, in some cases employing advertising pressures that may well have harmful effects upon societies' existing domestic and social patterns – like the fracas caused over Cow and Gate milk advertisements some few years ago. He will need to get into focus (if this is possible) some of the complex *political* problems that the new nations are facing; this will mean blurring and receding certain images, particularly those associated with the colonial period, and sharpening others, as countries experiment with new political formulae. And some of those new political formulae which will insist on stealing the centre of his vision may be those with which he is unfamiliar or even unsympathetic, but he will have to recognise that the subjects have changed and the new groups may not be those he would have anticipated, had he been taking the portraits fifteen or twenty years ago.

We could continue in this metaphor for some time, but the point should have been made clearly enough. This book urges an *informed sympathy* towards the Third World, and this information will need to be updated regularly. The Christian who wants to try to understand today's Third World scene will need to be alert to the media, and to use every available method to inform himself as to what is happening. For the Christian teacher this may well mean some imaginative restructuring of his curriculum, particularly if he is teaching in a multi-ethnic classroom[1]. He will want to avoid a totally Eurocentric curriculum and include some inputs of Indian, Caribbean and African history, geography and literature, emphasising the positive in each case. He will be anxious that one of his teaching objectives will be to open a new world of culture to his children, rectifying the myth that, for example, Africa was 'backward' and 'primitive' until the Europeans came to bring enlightenment to a dark continent[2], or that West Indian culture is totally dependent upon European influences[3].

Reference has already been made to the Christian's attitude towards men and women of different cultural backgrounds living in his own town. Clearly it is of vital importance that he should be as well informed about the cultural backgrounds of his Asian neighbours as possible, partly in order to be able to talk intelligently to them, but as well to help him to begin to understand just what the consequences are for the Hindu or the Muslim who forsakes his own religion and becomes a Christian. The point has already been made (page 93) that culture and religion are inextricably intertwined in Asian societies, and religion is not a private affair. If a Muslim becomes a Christian, this may well have a profound effect upon his standing within his society. So the Christian needs to appreciate what is implied when he asks his Muslim friend to abandon his own faith, and embrace the Christian faith.

In this connection, Christopher Lamb, the coordinator of the BCMS/CMS Other Faiths Theological Project, wrote a very thoughtful article in the *Evangelical Race Relations Group Journal* (Vol. 3 No. 5, April '79). He suggested that Christians must *stop* thinking of men and women of other religious groups living locally as a new kind of missionary challenge, because this immediately evokes certain attitudes and stances, notably those which imply that *we* (the Christians) are in a superior position to *them* (members of other faiths). Rather we should be much more personal in the way we approach people of other ethnic groups;

we meet people as ordinary people, all with human needs. The West has its areas of social and psychological poverty, and we would do well to look far more critically at the package of values – the belief that in some way Christianity, served with the trimmings of Western habits and norms, and communicated by means of all the advantages of our technological society, is the best fare to offer to those in the receiving position in the Third World. Rather we should approach evangelism as 'one beggar telling another beggar where to find bread'. We have found the bread of life in Christ (John 6:51) and this bread is to be shared and broken with all of our fellow men, whoever they may be or from whatever cultural background they may have come. But this sharing must not be seen by them 'as workhouse guardians seeking to imprison people in our institutions' (C. Lamb). Or to change the metaphor, the task of evangelism may be seen thus. 'The task, after removing the non-essential outer garments of our culture from the Gospel, is to reclothe it in the language and thoughtforms of those to whom we present it!'[4] Before leaving this metaphor, one is left wondering how suitable has been the Western style dress for displaying Christianity at its most attractive, and how much the West has attempted to force the body of Christ into clothes that do not show it to its best advantage. We do well to remember that the Christian Faith was born in the Middle East, that much of its imagery and illustration is Middle Eastern, and that its founder was no middle class English businessman!

It is not easy to find the point of balance between making a sympathetic effort to understand the cultures of other ethnic groups and appearing to accept the rightness of their religious beliefs. Certain church groups may quickly take up defensive positions.

Many Christians are not willing to engage in any form of dialogue which may be regarded as having 'interfaith' associations, while there are a few who would go still further and feel that active steps should be taken to *stop* other religious groups from worshipping in this our Christian country. For the thinking Christian, however, interfaith is not synonymous with syncretism; it may mean listening to other groups more sympathetically and accepting common ground if and where it exists.

Wolverhampton Inter-Faith Group, for example, produced a programme and calendar of religious festivals, detailing both Christian and other faith's special meetings, including (in 1978), an 'inter-faith bus tour' when a group were given a guided bus tour of four or five different places or worship. The aims and objectives of the group are clearly set out at the beginning of the book:

FULL STATEMENT OF AIMS

...to encourage and promote understanding and friendship between people of Wolverhampton whatever their religion.

...to work for racial harmony and peaceful co-existence in our multi-cultural town and oppose racial prejudice wherever it exists.

...to promote dialogue about faith, religious beliefs and customs, whilst honouring the integrity of believers, whatever their convictions.

...to endeavour to help minority groups where problems arise concerning needs requiring local government co-operation, or knowledge of community resources.

...to acknowledge with thankfulness agreed standards and codes of behaviour but to accept with honesty and respect fundamental religious or cultural differences.

The Gravesend Inter-Faith group also holds regular meetings, and in 1980 organised a day tour of Southall, as well as visits to a number of churches and temples in the area. Two outstanding occasions in 1980 were an Easter Celebration and a banquet to celebrate the end of Ramadan.

It is the writer's experience that such organisations do provide a valuable platform for dialogue and understanding. There is no attempt made to dilute one's Christian beliefs, but rather to *understand* the other person's creed. And this can be only for the good of all concerned. Perhaps the preceding chapters might have engendered some ideas that have at least started that process of understanding.

Another area where Christians can build bridges of friendship concerns overseas students living in Britain. Every town that has an institution of further or higher education is bound to have some overseas students, and in some of the larger towns where they are both Universities and Colleges of Further Education the number of overseas students may well run into some hundreds. In fact there are 50,000 overseas students living in Greater London alone. They come to this country to study for a wide variety of courses, although more come to read for qualifications in further education or degrees in the sciences, engineering and medicine than in the arts. Some live in College hostels, but the majority have to find their own accommodation, either in bedsits or in overseas students' hostels, like the Alliance Club or the Lee Abbey Overseas Students' Hostel in West London, both of which are under Christian management. Some overseas students are quite wealthy and are better off than their native counterparts, but these are a minority. The vast majority of overseas students have had to leave their families at home, and often find their stay in Britain lonely and unwelcoming. For many, their stay in this country is disillusioning, in that they come expecting a 'Christian country', but all too often they leave without making contact with Christians in a live and friendly church. Instead they are exposed to the pornography, materialism, and general atmosphere of unfriendliness of our large cities.

The Universities and Colleges Christian Fellowship has established an overseas Students' Department to help overseas students find a welcome here in Britain and in many cases to find the Saviour. Each August/September a 'welcome' programme is arranged when Christian students meet new arrivals, show them some of the tourist attractions of London and help them settle in. The UCCF bought 5 Doughty Street, London WC1 in 1965 and made this into a home for sixteen overseas students. The building is used also for Bible Studies and discussion groups and informal supper parties.

Christians can help by linking overseas students they know to the UCCF (contact Bryan Knell, UCCF Overseas Student Centre, 2 Newcombe Street, Kensington Place, London W8. Tel: 01 727 5010) and also by sharing in their hospitality scheme. Hundreds of overseas students visit Christian homes annually, either for a weekend visit or for a day, and in many cases this contact is the first that an overseas student will have with an English home. Needless to say he may well form his impressions of this country, and of the real meaning of the Christian faith, through this personal contact. It is no exaggeration to say that many overseas students return to positions of considerable influence in their home countries, and the strategic importance of this Christian contact cannot be overestimated.

The UCCF also organise church weekends for overseas students, when a local church will plan a programme for a group of twenty or more, taking them to local places of historical interest and then having an informal party in the evening. The students will then share in the Sunday morning worship services. Again the influence that such an experience can have on a student who is lonely and has begun to adopt a very cynical response to this country can be enormous. One African wrote of his visit to a Christian home in Kent, 'Thanks for the evening out, when we attended the outreach by the Mary Sisters. They set me thinking on one's need for Christ.' And this comment could be repeated hundreds of times, as overseas students find that it can be quite hospitable inside the forbidding walls of the Englishman's castle!

Although most overseas students are courteous enough not to register alarm when English hosts may expose not only their ignorance, but also their prejudices, when talking about the Third World, it would obviously be far better if their hosts were to some extent informed about the countries from which their guests have come. This book may help provide the kind of information that can facilitate meaningful communication with overseas students; indeed it may suggest the idea of organising a church-based overseas students weekend. Readers interested in this idea are urged to contact 2 Newcombe Street for further information.

I have left to last the matter of sharing our resources with men and women in the Third World, partly because it is of utmost importance, and also because some major theological and practical issues are raised when this matter is considered from a biblical standpoint.

For many in this country thinking about the Third World follows a fairly clearly plotted path. It starts with the knowledge of Third World poverty, argues that most of those who live there are not willing, or are not intelligent enough, to do anything about it. The British government rather unwillingly doles out some aid, and all we get back is a kick in the teeth from a local politician anxious to ingratiate himself with his people. And there's gratitude for you! At least it is to be hoped that this book has helped show the fallacies behind that line of thinking! But rich Christians cannot go on living in an age of hunger without taking some decisive action, firmly based on scriptural principles.

But what action? I have in front of me as I write Sider's disturbing book *Rich Christians in an Age of Hunger* with its powerful denunciation of the inequalities in the present world arena and its equally urgent plea for a simpler life style. I have also in front of me today's newspaper headlines, warning of the dramatic effects that the recent increases in crude oil prices will have upon our economy, and also reminding me of the growing pool of unemployed people in Britain, and I know that somehow I have to reconcile these three ever present facts; the fact that on this very day about 500 million men, women and children are either starving or eating a totally inadequate diet; the fact that I am living in a society whose existence in its present form is tied to certain raw materials; and the fact that I have to learn to live with inflation and employment uncertainty. This process of reconciliation is not easy. It is equally facile on the one hand to shrug one's shoulders and regard the dilemma as all too difficult to solve, and salve our consciences by increasing our contribution to Christian Aid next year; yet, on the other hand it is totally unrealistic to opt out of the culture and society in which we live, ignoring our responsibilities to our families as we run for the nearest Christian commune, using it as a bolt-hole to escape having to wrestle with the problem for ourselves.

Rather than attempt to offer a simple blueprint for all Christians to follow, I have made a list of some biblical principles that may help us to reach our conclusions.

1. God requires radically transformed economic relationships as well as transformed human and social behaviour, from his people! Economic exploitation, which is *one*, but not the *only* cause of inequalities in income and living standards, is part of the result of the fall, and the redeemed of the Lord will recognise this fact. It may be questionable as to how much we can do in protest against the exploitation of the Third World by the West in underpricing the primary products they export to us, or by putting tariffs on the commodities that they can produce more cheaply than we can, but at least we should not grumble when the price of coffee goes up, because farmers in East Africa and Latin America are paid more for their produce. There may well be readers who work in the Third World and who employ Third World nationals in business or at home. One would hope that they will see the rightness of paying them well above the minimum wage, and building a different quality of relationship with them from that practised by those who are not Christians. There may equally well be readers whose business is in international trade, and perhaps the following words written by the Brazilian Archbishop Dom Helder Camara should be sellotaped firmly on their desks:

It is not aid that we need...If the affluent countries of the East and West, Europe and the United States, are willing to pay fair prices to the developing countries for their natural resources, they can keep their aid and their relief plans.

Such a course of action will indeed be difficult for the Christian business man, because it will run counter to prevailing trade patterns, but perhaps the redeemed economic relationship he is seeking to establish with his clients in the Third World may well demand quite radical action.

Christian teachers who read this book will appreciate the need to reappraise certain areas in the curriculum. Among these may be some consideration of the ethics of international trade.

But before making quick value judgements as to why, e.g. India's textile trade has fallen behind that of Britain, it should be pointed out that when the East India Company first took over Bengal, her textile industry was more advanced than that in Britain. Britain reversed that direction by imposing a heavy import duty on Bengali textiles to Britain and by forcing Bengal to accept British textiles duty free. Nor is this situation confined to economic history; it is an ongoing one, as we are reminded from time to time in programmes such as *Panorama*, which take a critical look at the wage levels of (for example) tea workers in Sri Lanka or sugar cutters in the Caribbean that are paid by multi-national companies.

On the other hand, there are Christian thinkers who, no less concerned for their fellow believers in the Third World, see the role of multi-national companies as *beneficial* to development. They argue that the investment such companies stimulate provides employment for many, brings more people into the cash sector of the economy, and thus makes for a higher standard of living for many living in the Third World. And this is indeed true, so long as these companies *invest*, not *exploit* the people – and sometimes the line of demarcation is difficult to establish. Certainly codes of practice need to be established and rigidly adhered to on the part of multi-national companies trading in the Third World, to avoid the kind of exploitation that certainly has existed in the past.

It will be a skilful teacher who can encourage his pupils to think through these complex issues, but the Christian teacher should make sure that he is as well informed as possible, in order to tackle them in an informed manner with his students.

In 1974 the United Nations adopted a Charter of Economic Rights and Duties of States for the New International Economic

Order. Key proposals for action were passed in the following areas:

1. Prices of primary products and raw materials. These prices, the developing nations insisted, should increase immediately. Furthermore, the prices of these products should be tied directly to the prices of manufactured products which the poor nations have to import from rich nations.

   A common fund should be set up, which would be used to finance buffer stocks of twenty or thirty key commodities so that wild fluctuations in commodity prices could be ironed out.

2. Tariffs and other barriers to trade. Developed countries should remove tariffs and other trade barriers to products from the developing nations.

3. National sovereignty over national resources. This includes the right to nationalise foreign holdings with fair compensation.

4. Foreign aid. Rich nations should increase both emergency food aid and grants for long term development. The UN target of 0.7% of GNP on official development assistance by the developed countries should be achieved.

5. Patterns of industrial output. The developing world should increase its share of world manufactured goods output from about 10% in 1975 to 25% by the year 2000.

6. Debts should be rescheduled for many developing countries, and for the poorest it should be cancelled. (Many developing countries spend a large proportion of their current aid on meeting interest charges levied on aid previously received.)

7. There should be arrangements for the transfer of technology from developed to developing countries, other than through multi-national companies of which developing countries are very suspicious. (Quoted from *Rich Christians in an Age of Hunger* page 129).

This charter was again pressed for at the fourth UNCTAD Conference at Nairobi in 1976, and some limited progress was made towards setting up the Common Fund there and again at a subsequent meeting in Paris the following year. But progress has been very limited and Britain's total official aid figure in 1980 amounted to no more than £900 million – 0.34% of her GNP.[5] The projected ODA for 1981–82 is £1,037 million; this figure does not represent any increase in real money terms, but rather an allowance for inflation (at UK rates). In the present economic blizzard, there is virtually no chance of this Charter being taken seriously by the West.

I suggested above that it was questionable how much individual Christians can do to redress the unfair economic relationships between the West and the Third World.

That statement might itself have been too defeatist. We have a right to make our opinions known to our MPs and to express them in the press. When was the last occasion that any reader of this book lobbied his MP asking for Britain's aid to the developing world to be increased or wrote to the press in the same terms? The Festival of Light has campaigned against one social evil of our time. Is not economic greed an equally damaging activity? At least the Bishop of Southwark was prepared to express his concern; the *Guardian* (9th June 1979) reported that he had written to the Prime Minister earlier in the week pointing out that, whatever anti-inflationary measures she intended, aid to the Third World was a special case, concerning the plight of two-thirds of our fellow human beings, whose misery is out of all proportion to any minor hardships caused by the recession.

2. Jesus' Kingdom revolutionised many of the established norms and values, and instituted an entirely new set. These can be read in Matthew 5:1–12. In many cases these values are dramatically opposed to the world's standards; it is the humble, and not the self assertive, who are to be congratulated; the poor, and not the wealthy who are blest! And in the Kingdom of Heaven economic relationships, too, are transformed. The first citizens of this Kingdom shared their possessions; Jesus consistently taught them that they should enjoy a carefree attitude towards their possessions, and even their food and clothing (Matt. 6:25–33); in fact, he had no possessions, and even had no permanent home (Matt. 8:20). This basic desire to share became one of the key characteristics of the early Church, so much so that even non-Christians were impressed by it (Acts 2:32–37; Acts 4:43–47; Acts 5:11; Acts 6:1–7). The early Church followed this principle so faithfully that there was not a needy person among them (Acts 4:34). They enjoyed a oneness and closeness that we seem largely to have lost in subsequent generations. But it was a *koinonia* and a sharing that was based on *love* rather than *compulsion*. Ananias and Sapphira had no compulsion to sell their property; their sin was lying to God (Acts 5:4). Obviously some members of the early Church retained their own property – John Mark's mother Mary did, but put her home at the disposal

of the Church. And this attitude of sharing is to become part of our life-style. The use of the Greek imperfect tense in both Acts 2:45 and Acts 4:34 denotes a continued, repeated action over an extended period of time...'they often sold their possessions,' *not* 'they sold all their possessions as a single action.' This indicates, not a single 'one off' act of abolishing private property and living in a commune, but rather that the first Christians were happy to dispose of some of their assets when ever their fellow believers were in need.

Sider aptly describes their practice as one *of unlimited liability and total availability*:

> Their sharing was not superficial or occasional. Regularly and repeatedly, 'they sold their possessions and goods and distributed them to all, as any had need'. If the need was greater than current cash reserves, they sold property. They simply gave until the needs were met. The needs of the sister and brother, not legal property rights or future financial security, were decisive. They made their financial resources unconditionally available to each other. Oneness in Christ for the earliest Christian community meant unlimited economic liability for, and total economic availability to, the other members of Christ's Body (pages 90–91).

As Christian communities began to be established in many cities in the Roman world, so this attitude of sharing took on a new geographical dimension. When famine struck Palestine in AD 46, the believers at Antioch were quick to send relief. Paul was very concerned to encourage the new churches founded by his ministry to contribute towards the needs of the Jerusalem church (Rom. 15:25–28; 2 Cor. 7–9). *Koinonia* to Paul meant *fellowship with someone or participation in something*, and this sharing experience was best illustrated in the act of sharing the one bread and the common cup in the Lord's Supper. In fact Paul used the word *koinonia* to designate financial sharing among believers (1 Cor. 9:13; Rom. 15:26).

Of course it would be facile to suggest that we today should slavishly imitate every detail of the life of the early Church. But it is for us to set our lives by scriptural principles, and as we have seen in the above paragraphs, fellowship means sharing resources. Many Christians would argue that the present set up, where a small fraction of the world's Christians grow richer year by year while our brothers and sisters in the Third World suffer from lack of proper food, inadequate medical attention and the restricting effects of minimal education, is one direct result of man's sinful greed and a major hindrance to world evangelism. Certainly we have no option, if we want to follow the Lord's teaching, but to look again at his teaching on sharing and caring.

3. The Scriptures indicate very clearly that God has always been concerned for the poor. Jesus began his public ministry by identifying with the prophecy of Isaiah and announcing that:

> The Spirit of the Lord is upon me, because he has anointed me to preach good news to the poor. He has sent me to proclaim release to the captives and recovering of sight to the blind, to set at liberty those who are oppressed, to proclaim the acceptable year of the Lord (Luke 4:18–19).

Jesus' actual ministry corresponded precisely with those words. His followers were, by and large, poor men, and he spent most of his time preaching and healing in the cultural and economic backwater of Galilee, not with the rich and influential people in Jerusalem. He himself was a poor man and was buried in a borrowed tomb.

The corollary of this argument is also true. Clearly God does not hate the rich, but he is displeased with those who have become rich by exploiting the poor. No one can doubt this fact after reading sections of Amos! He denounced the rich women ('well fed cows') who got fat by illtreating the weak and oppressing the poor, and demanded that their husbands kept them well-stocked with liquor (Amos 4:1); he attacked those who meted out unfair justice in the courts (5:10–13) and sold the poor into slavery for a pair of shoes (2:6). Jeremiah was to speak in similar angry terms a hundred and fifty years later (Jer. 5:26–29). Perhaps the song of Mary is the most explicit outburst of God's care for the poor and the distaste of those who have become rich through exploiting the poor.

> He has stretched out his mighty arm and scattered the proud with all their plans. He has brought down mighty kings from their thrones and lifted up the lowly. He has filled the hungry with good things and sent the rich away with empty hands (Luke 1:51–53).

When Jesus outlined the radical and completely other worldly values of his new Kingdom, he announced:

> Blessed are you poor, for yours is the Kingdom of God. Blessed are

you that hunger now, for you shall be satisfied.... Woe to you that are rich for you have received your consolation. Woe to you that are full now, for you shall hunger (Luke 6:20–25).

Perhaps we should at this point in our survey of biblical attitudes towards wealth and poverty clear up two misconceptions that may have crept into some people's thinking. In the first place, God is not a Marxist. As we shall see in a subsequent paragraph, there is no biblical injunction against owning property, nor acquiring some degree of wealth (see page 115). God has no class favourites, nor does he love the poor more than the wealthy. Rather he hates and punishes injustice and neglect of the poor. The man who has possessions has a greater responsibility and a greater degree of stewardship to *share* his wealth, and never to increase his possessions by oppressing the poor. Secondly, it would be wrong to give the impression that God is 'on the side of the poor'. In *Rich Christians in an Age of Hunger* this tends to be something of a catch-phrase, (with the implication that he favours them over and against the rich). I do not find scriptural evidence to support this thesis; rather God is *concerned for* the poor and wills that there should be greater degrees of sharing among Christians.

4. The Bible does not teach absolute economic equality as an ideal in the Marxist sense. What it does teach consistently is the *principle of Christian stewardship*. The parable of the Talents (or the Three Servants, according to the Good News Bible) Matthew 25:14–30, or of the Gold Coins, Luke 19:11–27, both stress that the master rewarded the servants who had invested what they had been given. The corollary is even more startling; the man who failed to invest was punished for his laziness. In the one parable the three servants started off with vastly differing amounts (from many thousands of pounds to a handful of pounds, in modern equivalents); in the other they were all given the same amount. But in both cases the *point* of the parable is the same; they are expected to invest their talents and make a profit. I do not think this parable is intended to be taken only in a conceptualised, spiritual sense, implying that we should improve and use our skills and natural gifts. I believe that it also has a basic economic interpretation, and that we are expected to use whatever financial assets we have in a way designed to maximise their value, so long as those assets are first dedicated to God.

Christians are not born into environments that are completely equal – for all sorts of reasons. Differences in social environment, in educational opportunity and in employment are three obvious differences that make for inequalities in the resources that Christians possess. Thus, for example, a family living comfortably in a wealthy suburb of London or Manchester, owning two cars and sending their children to a private school, have very different responsibilities in terms of Christian stewardship from another family living, for example, in a council house in Glasgow, where the father is unemployed and the children receive free school meals. Similarly, a graduate who has had all the advantages of higher education and now holds an influential position in business or in a profession has a very different responsibility from somebody living at the other end of the town who has recently been made redundant. I do not believe that the wealthy family or the graduate are any less favoured in the Lord's sight than the unemployed Glaswegian or the man who has lost his job. But I do believe that the former pair should be willing to share, and share to the full, in terms of material possessions and time with the latter, particularly if they meet in fellowship. It would be a denial of *koinonia* for the pair living on the dole to go without while the business man has plenty. Clearly business family and graduate alike have greater responsibility *to use their talents* – their money, their cars, their home, their skills, their influence – to further the Kingdom of Heaven, and more will be expected of them. The faithful steward who was given charge of his master's household while he went away was rewarded for working well (Luke 12:42–48); Jesus underlined the principle of stewardship in his final comment on this parable. 'Much is required from the person to whom much is given; much more is required from the person to whom much more is given' (Luke 12:48).

This principle of the worthiness of Christian stewardship has almost been built up into a historical thesis. R. H. Tawney, for example, in his classic *Religion and the Rise of Capitalism* argued that there is a close correlation between Christian entrepreneurs and the rise of the monied class. The sixteenth century Puritans turned their backs on frivolity and many became 'the new gentry' of the early seventeenth century, preferring to use their time in furthering their businesses. A number of the great industrial magnates of the nineteenth century were non-conformists, who, partly because they were politically less favoured than their Anglican counterparts, and partly because of their conviction that a hard honest day's work honoured the Lord, devoted their energies to working hard and in consequence made a lot of money. In the twentieth century, one could cite men like the late Sir John Laing who have adopted the same philosophy. The Christian Brethren, for example, include a number of wealthy men who have indeed been very successful stewards of their financial resources. The key point to make in this context, however, is that many of these have been extremely generous in endowing Christian institutions. London Bible College was greatly assisted in its early days by the generosity of three wealthy Christian business men – Philip Henman, Sir John Laing and Ernest Bartlett. This is of course, only one isolated example of the generosity of Christians in helping Christian causes in England and overseas. To be wealthy, therefore, does not in itself constitute sin. It is the *love of money* which Paul warns Timothy against, because that temptation can indeed cause havoc to one's faith (1 Tim. 6:10). And perhaps we should remind ourselves that a man (or woman) must be careful lest his (or her) investment is exploitative. Is he underpaying for goods bought from the Third World – or from the poor in this country for that matter? Is he paying his employees a generous wage, showing genuine concern for their welfare? Does he use his profit in a disciplined sense?

5. If the Bible indicates that careful stewardship and wise investment of our resources is to be practised, even more does it emphasise the need *to maintain a carefree attitude* towards our possessions. It is one thing to be thoughtful about the way we use, and sometimes invest our resources; it is a very different matter to worry about them. When Jesus introduced his new Kingdom to his first followers, he must have amazed, if not confused them, by some of the things he suggested! To tell them, for example, not to worry about how they fed or clothed themselves any more than the birds think about these things must have seemed completely otherworldly. But he did:

> I bid you put away anxious thoughts about food to keep you alive and clothes to cover your body. Life is more than food, the body more than clothes. Think of the ravens; they neither sow nor reap; they have no storehouse or barn; yet God feeds them. You are worth far more than the birds! Is there a man among you who by anxious thought can add a foot to his height? If, then you cannot do even a very little thing, why are you anxious about the rest?
>
> Think of the lilies of the field; they neither spin nor weave; yet I tell you even Solomon in all his splendour was not attired like one of

these. But if that is how God clothes the grass, which is growing in the field today, and tomorrow is thrown on the stove, how much more will he clothe you! How little faith you have! And so you are not to set your mind on food and drink; you are not to worry. For all these things are for the heathen to run after; but you have a Father who knows that you need them. No, set your mind upon his Kingdom, and all the rest will come to you as well (Luke 12:22–31).

And he reinforced that lesson on a number of occasions (Matt. 6:24; Luke 12:33–34; Luke 18:24–25).

It isn't easy for a Christian to be rich. He has to work out how he should best use his wealth; he has to know in what ways, and under what circumstances it is appropriate to invest it – and he has always to be on his guard against worrying about it! The Greek word translated 'covetousness' (*pleonexia*) means 'striving for material possessions', and this was precisely what the rich fool did (Luke 12:16–21). The farmer in this parable was not wrong to build bigger barns, because this would have been a prudent decision to take and accords well with our agreed principle of wise stewardship. His sins were rather a total lack of concern for the needy who might have lived near him, and a total neglect of his spiritual responsibility towards God.

We have already recognised that the matter of reaching a simpler life style that is both sciptural and practicable in this day and age is no easy task, and this complexity is largely the result of the society in which we live. Certain elements within our own society *do* pressurize us into a preoccupation with material goods, whether they can be colour TV sets, more comfortable cars, sun-drenched beaches where we can be sure of a sun-tan (and who can deny that a cold week sitting on a British beach can leave us more frustrated than before we began our holiday?), or even better quality cat food. A missionary friend on leave from Zaïre was shattered to be reminded from a large hoarding in her local shopping area that 'every cat has a *right* to eat fish!' It would be very difficult indeed to become totally impervious to the barrage of advertising pressure that is going on around us, and we begin to succumb to the temptation to all the world 'to squeeze us into its mould' (Romans 12:1–2, J. B. Phillips) and to become preoccupied with material things.

As a Christian, I am anxious to follow my Lord's teaching and to allow him to transform my values and norms – and become a true citizen of his Kingdom. I know that Jesus urged his disciples to enjoy a carefree attitude towards possessions. I am equally aware of the danger of the sin of covetousness. But I cannot totally escape from the pressures of the society in which I live, and the TV will not conveniently 'fade out' those commercials which it feels might tempt me! Perhaps even more relevant is the fact that I know that I have to face up to quite legitimate demands upon my resources. As I write I know that, once my present appointment terminates, I shall have to move house. House prices are escalating, and my growing family demands more playing space. If I am to work and write usefully, I shall have to acquire a study where I can shut myself away from my family. If I do not acquire a garage, my car will collapse into a rust heap. The list could be extended. I like my wife to wear an attractive dress when I take her out and I know that it is important for her to feel attractive and not to accept lower standards of personal appearance than her non-Christian friends would tolerate.

Most of us face similar circumstances. It might be easier if we could opt out of having to make these difficult decisions and go to live in some sort of commune, handing over our financial responsibilities to somebody else. But this would be irresponsible behaviour. Jesus' Kingdom is here and now, and he expects us to live out his new life-style in such a way that even those who are not Christians are impressed and glorify him because of our behaviour (Matt. 5:16). And one important aspect of this new life-style is to learn a new carefree yet responsible attitude towards our possessions.

6. We may well need to think very seriously about adopting a simpler life-style. In 1974 the International Congress on World Evangelism held at Lausanne came to grips with a number of vital issues in the contemporary world. One quite new and very disturbing contribution came from the voice of churches in the Third World, heard in a way that many church leaders in the West had never before bothered to listen to. It was clear that many churches in the Third World have acquired some of the gifts that Western Christendom has largley lost. Their ranks include some of the finest preachers and the most gifted evangelists, as well as some of the deepest and most compelling thinkers in Christendom. And these men are *theologically* concerned about the gulf between Christians in the West and those living in many parts of the Third World. They brought their concern to the attention of the Congress, and one of the final resolutions was as follows:

Those of us who live in affluent circumstances accept our duty to develop a simpler life-style in order to contribute more generously to both relief and evangelism.

One of the inescapable conclusions of this study is that we in the West need to take more seriously the real meaning of economic *koinonia*. We cannot go on enjoying a richer life-style while 10,000 persons die each day because of inadequate food. I think few Christians would not readily accept this fact; the problem is how to go about sharing what we have in such a way that our giving is disciplined and yet spontaneous, and that the money and resources we give are wisely used, for sometimes it would be quite inappropriate merely to give more money to the poor of the Third World. The Oxfam poster that suggests that it would be much more sensible *to teach a man to fish than to give him a fish* is absolutely right. So where do we go from here?

I have already offered some suggestions regarding possible *public* action that Christians in this country may take in order to protest against some of the structural evils of our day in terms of relationships between the West and the Third World (page 115). Meaningful action may involve Christian businessmen in reconsidering some of their business practices, and in particular the quality of trading relationships, in terms of fair prices and reasonable wages, they share with their clients in the Third World. This kind of action may well prove costly to Christians in business, and may indeed also cost them popularity, as their non-Christian business colleagues find these biblical attitudes unfamiliar and hard to accept. Certainly the Christian teacher will want to have a careful look at his curriculum and make sure that he is sufficiently informed to be able to teach such topics as international aid and trade, world food supplies and distribution as well as some of the current problems that newly independent countries in the Third World are facing, in a well informed and sympathetic way. All this will require a fair amount of extra reading. He also needs to offer a *positive image* of the Third World, not concentrating only on those aspects that reinforce 'the poverty cycle', but teaching also some of the exciting contributions to art and society that Third World countries have made.[6] The primary schoolteacher is in a specially fortunate position here, in that the colour and variety of Third World culture is virtually unknown to children of this age; it is just waiting to be explored.

It is scarcely necessary to add that the thoughtful minister should ensure that his congregation is well taught in the theology of giving, and is also made aware of some of the major issues that have been considered in this book. But is this actually happening? When did your minister last lead a Bible study on any of the major topics raised in this book? And, lest we fall into the trap of thinking that we can conveniently pass the responsibility onto his shoulders – when did your house group last discuss them?[7]

But in the last analysis the response must be an individual one. The measure of our commitment to our Lord must to a considerable degree be evidenced by the extent to which we are prepared to share with our fellow Christians in need. Perhaps some guidelines will help focus our thinking. Firstly, we need to take to ourselves the recommendation of the Lausanne Covenant quoted above and press on with the adoption of a simpler life-style. Clearly this will involve steeling ourselves against the subtle influences of commercial advertising, and (even more difficult) the insidious temptation to keep up with the Joneses'! To quote again from *Rich Christians in an Age of Hunger*:

> we Christians need to make some dramatic, concrete moves to escape the materialism that seeps into our minds via the clever and incessant TV commercials. We have been brain washed to believe that bigger houses, more prosperous businesses and more luxurious gadgets are worthy goals in life. As a result, we are caught in an absurd, materialistic spiral. The more we make, the more we think we need in order to live decently and respectably. Somehow we have to break this cycle because it makes us sin against our needy brothers and sisters and therefore, against our Lord.

It would be wrong for one Christian to lay down inflexible rules that all other Christian people should follow in reaching a simpler life-style. Sider's 'Three Year rule' (he reckons to buy a new outfit every three years, and then feels guilty if he breaks that rule, because the money he spent on buying a new suit could have fed a starving child in India for about a year) may or may not be right for me. It would be quite wrong to gauge a Christian's spirituality by the number of new clothes he or she buys. Each Christian operates under a different set of circumstances, and it may be a necessary part of a person's work situation always to dress smartly. But this does not alter the fact that many of us could easily cut back on our expenditure on clothes and thereby increase our giving.

Other areas in our life-style at which we could well look critically are furniture, cars and holidays. We are tempted to buy a new suite of furniture as soon as our present suite shows the first sign of wear, although this outlay is frequently unnecessary. Motoring costs are becoming excessively high, and although many of us who own a car would rightly affirm that we use it in the Lord's service, we need to think very carefully before trading it in for a new model, rationalising our action by quoting the growing cost of repairs on an older vehicle. We do need to get a proper holiday each year, in order to recharge our emotional batteries as well as to give our bodies a rest, but I'm not sure that the argument that we shall appreciate the Gospel narrative better if we can take our holiday in the Holy Land is a very biblical one!

Sider offers a check list of twelve practical suggestions that Christians might use when working our revisions in their own life-style. Bear in mind that the checklist was originally written for an American readership, that some priorities and norms are different from ours, and that some suggestions may be more practicable than others, then work through the list thoughtfully. It should at least stimulate further thought and discussion.

PRACTICAL SUGGESTIONS (Quoted from *Rich Christians in an Age of Hunger*, pp. 157–8.) The following are hints, not rules. Freedom, joy and laughter are essential elements of simple living.

1. Reduce your food budget by:
   a. gardening; try hoeing instead of mowing; how about getting an allotment?
   b. substituting vegetable protein for animal protein.
   c. setting a monthly budget and sticking to it.

2. Question your own life-style, not your neighbours!

3. Lower energy consumption by:
   a. keeping your thermostat (at the home and office) at 65°F or lower during winter months; and only heat the rooms you are using.
   b. using public transport. It's also much safer!
   c. using bicycles, carpools and, for trips under one mile, your feet.
   d. making dish-washing a family time instead of buying a dishwasher.

4. Resist TV advertising by:
   a. turning down the sound, when commercials come on and

using the time to do something else, or talk about the programme you are watching.

5. Buy and renovate an old house in the inner city (and persuade a
   few friends to do the same so you can form a Christian
   community).

6. Reduce our society's consumption of non-renewable natural resources by:
   a. resisting planned obsolescence (purchasing quality products
      when you must buy).
   b. sharing appliances, tools, lawnmowers, sports equipment,
      books, even a car (this is easier if you live close to other
      Christians committed to simple living).
   c. asking whether a car is really essential for you.
   d. organising a 'things closet' in your church for items used only
      occasionally – edger, clippers, camp beds for unexpected
      guests, lawnmowers, camping equipment, ladder.

7. Have one or two 'home-made' babies and then adopt.

8. See how much of what you spend is for status and eliminate it.

9. Refuse to keep up with clothes fashions.

10. Find out what the supplementary benefit level is for you and your
    family and try living on it for three months.

11. Give your children and relations more of your love and time
    rather than more things.

12. Question all items of your expenditure.

But we do well to remember that there is no virtue in working
towards a simpler life-style *simply for its own sake*. There is no
intrinsic virtue in asceticism; this is not a Protestant ethic. We
are in the business of discovering ways in which each individual
reader works out some specific, concrete plan whereby he or she
can share to a greater extent than previously his resources with
his brothers and sisters who are in urgent need of food, medicine
and education. Once we have worked out a programme whereby
we can live more simply, then we have to decide upon a new
strategy for giving. Again it would be quite wrong for me to offer
hard and fast rules to be adopted unthinkingly by all Christian
people. Individuals' circumstances or commitments differ enormously, and these differences have to be taken into account.

Many Christians have adopted the tithe as a basic rule of
thumb for their Christian giving. Certainly there is good scriptural foundation for this (Gen. 28:22). But we need to appreciate

that even this generally accepted principle must be regarded as a flexible one. A Christian family with an income of £5,000 a year will find the £500 they give to the Lord's work a much greater measure of financial committment than another family who tithe an income of £15,000, for the obvious reason that the residual £13,500 will go a lot further than the former family's £4,500. As one's salary climbs the incremental and promotional ladder, so additional increases become less necessary in order to maintain one's basic living standards, and are used rather to purchase more luxury goods. Often a marked rise in income leads to a change of life-style, as the family exchange their small three bedroomed semi-detached house for a four bedroomed detached residence, drive a larger car, and indulge in more expensive hobbies like horse riding or sailing. And thus a new spiral of demand is created, as these more expensive items have to be financed!

Some have adopted the *graduated tithe*. A family must first sit down and work out an income that they need, to live at a reasonable, although not luxurious standard of living, for the coming year. Having reached that figure, they covenant to tithe that figure. For every additional £250 above that basic amount, they increase their giving by 5% (or 2%) depending on their circumstances. The table below illustrates how this plan works out for a family with an income of £8,000 per annum.

Basic living income for a family with 3 children at school – £8,000

Income		Percentage giving	Actual amount given
First	£7,000	10%	£700
Next	250	15% (12%)	37.50 (£30)
Next	250	20% (14%)	50.00 (35)
Next	250	25% (16%)	62.00 (40)
Next	250	30% (18%)	75.00 (45)
Total Income	£8,000	Total Given	£925.00 (£850)

(The figures in brackets indicate the lower increases in the graduated tithe. The figure of £8,000 regarded as 'basic living income' was based upon 1980 figures, and may be totally unrealistic by the time this paragraph is read).

This suggestion may commend itself more to some than to others, and is meant only as a starting point for further consideration and discussion. But the key principle is for giving to be *regular, disciplined* and *systematic.* Do not wait until February before dispatching deeds of covenant for the current tax year! The chances are that there will not be sufficient funds available to meet these, and then one gets in arrears. Better take out monthly or quarterly bankers orders, so the deductions are relatively painless!

Secondly, one needs to revise the figures regularly. Deeds of covenant taken out to enable a church or missionary society to reclaim the basic rate of income tax have to be made for either a four or a seven year period. By about year four of a seven year covenant the amount originally covenanted may well have only 75% of the purchasing power it had when the covenant was originally made. This difficulty can be remedied by taking out subsequent covenants, in order to boost the original amount to take inflation into account.

It would be very difficult in a book of this kind to suggest specific ways in which money is given; individual's interests are so varied. Some churches in this country are now working towards an overall budget, so that the church treasurer acts as an 'agent' and sends donations to various missionary societies on behalf of the church. Others prefer to retain their own links with missionary societies of their choice. Obviously one wants to be sure that one's money is being wisely used, and I suppose the criteria for this will include the extent to which the money is used to help others help themselves – to teach the people to fish, rather than merely give them fish. This may call for some heart-searching on the part of those who have lovingly given to small missionary societies that should perhaps amalgamate with larger ones and thus reduce administrative overheads. Many favour the personalised approach, like supporting a particular missionary or supporting a child in the Third World. Tear Fund is one society that has introduced a scheme like this, and the donor receives news of his adopted child from time to time.

At the end of the day three facts remain. While we ponder what to do next, 10,000 more people die each die for lack of food, and many thousands more are under-nourished, stunted, and with life expectations that would ensure that many who read this sentence would have to consider making their funeral arrangements with all possible speed, if they lived in many parts of the Third World. Poverty, in its fullest sense, is a reality in many parts of the Third World. The second fact concerns our standard of living in the West. Despite the escalating price of oil and its many related by-products, we are becoming a more affluent and pleasure-loving society. Thirdly, we who love and serve the Lord Jesus have a scriptural responsibility towards our fellow-believers. The principle of unconditional availability and unlimited liability for those of our brothers and sisters in need is a New Testament principle – *koinonia* means sharing something with someone. This scriptural teaching is still relevant in the twentieth century. And the task of applying this principle in an unequal but very complex world will demand some careful thought and must then lead to positive action on our part.

I set out determined not to fall into the trap of writing yet another book pleading for more money for the Third World. Some would point out that I have done just that. If so, the book will have partly miscarried in its intentions. The Third World is so complex, and any understanding of it must take into account the enormous contrasts found there between poverty and wealth, backwardness and sophistication, and between ignorance and advanced technology. In terms of religious commitment, the Third World includes pagans and animists, men and women who adhere to other religious beliefs – Muslims, Hindus, Sikhs, Buddhists and others – and also millions of born-again Christians. If this book has served to highlight some of these contrasts, and to throw some light on the kaleidoscope of economic strategies, political experiments, new and original educational strategies and above all on the emergence of an exciting and rapidly growing church in the Third World, then it has succeeded in its object. Poverty there is, but let us also look at the *wealth* of the Third World, not only in terms of art and music, but much more in terms of a spiritual vitality for which many of us in this country long. The Church in the Third World can teach the Church of the West a great deal about real Christian living in the 1980s.

Epilogue

A critic reading this book could quickly point out that it represents yet another attempt by a well-meaning European to put the Third World to rights, and that the author himself, like the missionary societies he has criticised, has been conditioned by Western values and priorities. To some extent this criticism is irrefutable: it is impossible totally to disengage onself from one's culture and environment. But at least I have been aware of this danger, and, in order to give a genuine Third World flavour to the text, talked at length to a group of ten overseas students representing seven independent countries in the three Third World continents. Many of their thoughts have been interwoven into Chapters Three and Four, but I concluded my discussion with the group by asking each member if there was one specific message they, potential Christian leaders from the Third World, would want to say to us, British Christians, anxious to gain a more accurate and balanced view of the tasks their churches face in the eighties. Their answers were very telling, and to my mind form a fitting conclusion to this book.

Two students indicated that the first priority the Third World church needs in the eighties is for *good leadership* – leadership appropriate to local needs. New churches need *both* clear and firm leadership in the sense of efficient administration and clear-cut planning policies, *and* a high calibre of spiritual leadership, as Christian leaders face some of the dilemmas outlined in Chapter Four. For some, this will involve knowing how to accommodate new political and economic structures as they emerge locally: when should they encourage the Christian community to support new policies and when, for the sake of the Gospel, should they oppose them? When should they involve the church in the political arena and when should they remain silent?

Faced with massive and complex decisions, Christian leadership needs to be properly trained and obviously capable, so that its calibre can match the strong political leadership commonly exercised in the Third World today. Obviously this leadership needs to be in national hands, but none of the students to whom I spoke regarded the role of expatriate missionaries as superflous in the Third World in the eighties; rather they should regard themselves as servants of the local church, not still as agents of the West.

One student warned me of the risk of adopting patronising attitudes in my approach to the Third World and its problems. I hope sincerely that I have avoided taking such a stance, even ingenuously, because nothing could be more insulting to our brothers and sisters in Christ than to be the subject of yet another 'kindly' downward glance on the part of another European, spelling out all their problems as *he* sees them, or giving faint praise when *he* thinks they have achieved progress.

This final paragraph was written on the train returning home from the exciting, if somewhat noisy, celebration sponsored in January 1980 by British Youth for Christ – *Our God Reigns*. This moving and Spirit-filled occasion seemed to me to encapsulate the new calibre of relationship between Christians from the Third World and those from Britain. The occasion was clearly a British one, led by well-known figures like Graham Kendrick, Dave Pope and Clive Calver. But the challenging final message, listened to in intense silence by 5,000 young people, was given by Luis Palau, Argentinian evangelist, who challenged his audience to enter the eighties by giving to God every aspect of their lives.

It would be wonderful if this kind of experience could become a feature of the Church in Britain in this decade, as something of the exuberance and freshness of the Third World evangelists is injected into our worship and evangelism.

The Church in Britain has an enormous bank of resources, both in terms of spiritual understanding and of practical experience to offer to its brothers and sisters in Christ in the Third World. It has also theological learning, expressed in a vast library of books written by very many scholars who are themselves deeply committed Christians, and has evolved a variety of forms of expression and worship. It has theological and missionary training colleges, staffed by godly men and women, many of whom have themselves worked alongside local Christians in the Third World.

Much of this fund of experience and wisdom the new churches in the Third World need in the eighties. But they must be given the right to select from the West those lessons most suited to their own situations. What is more, they have every right to hammer these out on the anvil of their own experiences and circumstances, so that the shape that emerges is right for each local church.

Suggestions for further reading

Brandt, W. *North-South: A Programme for Survival – Report of the Brandt Commission*. (Pan Books 1980). Two summaries are available:
a. *Programme for Survival* – a 4 page leaflet (12p plus postage)
b. *North-South: our links with the poorer countries of the world* (18p plus postage).
Both can be obtained, together with a full catalogue of teaching aids, resource materials etc. for use in schools, from: Centre for World Development, 128 Buckingham Palace Road, London SW1.

Cotterill, P. *The Eleventh Commandment* (IVP 1981). A thoughtful study of missiology, written by the Director of Overseas Studies at London Bible College.

Goldsmith, Martin *Don't Just Stand There!* (IVP 1976). An introduction to the biblical basis for outreach.

Harrison, Paul *Inside the Third World* (Penguin). 'For the novice, a quick primer into a complex subject: for the specialist it is full of fresh insights' (New Society).
Harrison, Paul *The Third World Tomorrow* (Pelican 1980). Very readable report on how 'self help', small-scale appropriate technologies and other concepts are being put into practice in Asia, Africa and Latin America.
Hastings, Adrian *A History of African Christianity 1950–75* (Cambridge African Studies series). Deals with the subject under three headings: Church and State, The Historic Churches, and Independence.

Kirk, J. A. *Liberation Theology: An Evangelical View from the Third World* (Marshall, Morgan & Scott 1980). The first serious work written by an evangelical to explain the significance of Latin-American liberation theology.

Lean, Geoffrey *Rich World, Poor World* (Allen & Unwin 1978). Quite a serious study of the main issues raised in Chapter Two, and will

133

certainly repay careful reading. Includes a very thoughtful chapter on urbanisation in the Third World.

Mountjoy, A. (Ed.) *The Third World; Problems and Perspectives* (Macmillan 1978). A series of very useful chapters, written by specialists, dealing with all the matters raised in Chapter Two, as well as some not mentioned, e.g. industrialisation and the Third World, intermediate technology etc.

Reed, Andrew *The Developing World* (Bell & Hyman 1979). A response is the growing interest in teaching about development at 'O' level. Excellently illustrated with photographs and maps and plenty of exercises for students.

Sider, Ronald J. *Rich Christians in an Age of Hunger – A Biblical Study* (Hodder & Stoughton 1978). Compelling reading: even though one may not agree with all the conclusions reached, it very effectively highlights an area of Christian responsibility hitherto largely neglected. Sider has also edited *Living More Simply – Biblical Principles and Practical Models* (Hodder 1980), a symposium from a group of American theologians and writers. Challenging and thought-provoking.

   Crusade has produced two excellent Study and Action Guides, one entitled *Hard Questions for Rich Christians*, based on Sider's book. This pamphlet offers an excellent summary of *Rich Christians in an Age of Hunger*, section by section, and each of the four sections includes a number of questions for group discussion. The questions are by no means uncritical and focus clearly on the main issues Sider raises. Strongly recommended for readers interested in the topics discussed in this book. Available at 10p from Crusade, 130 City Road, London EC1V 2NJ, or Tear Fund Publications Department, 11 Station Road, Teddington, Middlesex TW11 9AH.

   The other *Crusade* supplement, also at 10p, is called *Enough is as Good as a Feast*, and deals with a similar topic. This supplement preceded the publication of *Rich Christians in an Age of Hunger*.

Sinclair, M. *Green Finger of God* (Paternoster 1980). A first-hand account of a development project in the Argentinian Chaco; simultaneously an essay in development theology.

Singer, H. and Ansaur, J. *Rich and Poor Countries* (2nd edition) (Allen & Unwin 1978).

Sookhdeo, P. (Ed.) *Jesus Christ the Only Way* (Paternoster 1978). Some excellent chapters in this book, offering invaluable material on living in our multi-cultural society here in Britain.

Stamp, E. (Ed.) *Growing Out of Poverty* (Oxford 1977). A symposium describing positive steps that have been made to improve resources in the Third World. Chapter headings include 'Crops',

'Nuitrition' and 'Organisation'.

There are a number of school textbooks on the Third World. Teachers can visit CWDE, SOAS and the Commonwealth Institute Libraries to see what resources are available to help them.

Tear Fund produce some very useful material, ideal for stimulating thought among church groups and in schools. Among recent productions are a 'Food for Thought' target pack, and a filmstrip – the latter available either for purchase or on loan. Full catalogues of their publications are available from Tear Fund at 11 Station Road, Teddington, Middlesex TW11 9AH.

Some Organisations involved in Development Programmes

Catholic Institute for International Relations (CIIR). Independent Catholic organisation which promotes understanding within the United Kingdom on International relations, particularly overseas development. It publishes material suitable for use with adult groups, and produces a regular newsbrief, Comment, on issues of current international importance, and *CIIR News Quarterly*. 1 Cambridge Terrace, London NW1 4JL.

Centre for World Development Education (CWDE). Independent educational organisation whose aim is to increase knowledge and understanding in Britain of world development and the developing countries. CWDE publishes a wide range of written and visual materials and has recently published a series of reports of working parties recommending ways in which school curricula may include a greater Third World input. Teachers will find their resources centre extremely useful. 128 Buckingham Palace Road, London SW1. Tel: 01 730 8332/3.

Christian Aid. Official development and relief agency of the British Council of Churches. It offers (free and for sale) publications, posters, simulation games, filmstrips and films. Catalogues free. PO Box No. 1, London SW9 8BH.

Commonwealth Institute. This houses a permanent exhibition depicting many aspects of life in all forty-six Commonwealth countries, using effective display techniques. An education staff teach classes of children at the Institute using artefacts and visual aids to illustrate their lessons. There is also an excellent library and resources centre. Teachers anxious to include a greater Third World input into their lessons would be well advised to visit the Institute. Kensington High Street, London W8. Tel: 01 602 3252.

Commonwealth Secretariat. The Secretariat is responsible to and financed by the forty-six independent nations of the Commonwealth, and is the main instrument of multilateral cooperation between them. It provides technical assistance, advisers, experts and training to Commonwealth developing countries. Free publications list from Information Office, Marlborough House, London SW1Y 5HX.

Evangelical Missionary Alliance. A 'think tank' on mission and missionaries; holds an annual conference of member societies at High Leigh. The EMA is aware of the problems of mission reorientation and is seeking to find strategies to bring societies together. Whitefield House, 186 Kennington Park Road, London SE11 4BT.

Evangelical Race Relations Group. Seeks to bring together Christians concerned to reach a Christian viewpoint on race relations and the churches' response to our multi-ethnic society. Secretary: Miss Dorothy McQuaker, 57 Luke House, Bigland Street, London E1. Tel: 01 790 1770.

The Haselmere Group. Independent voluntary organisation founded in 1968 to discuss the social and economic crisis facing the developing countries. The Group welcomes postal enquiries and new members. C/o 467 Caledonian Road, London N7 9BE.

Help the Aged. Help the Aged seeks to promote the welfare of the elderly in Britain and the Third World, both by fund raising and by public campaigning. Posters, wall charts, booklets and other publications, films and slides. Callers welcome. 32 Dover Street, London W1A 2AP.

The Institute of Development Studies (IDS). The Institute of Development Studies was set up by ODM in 1966 as a national centre concerned with Third World development and with the relationships between rich and poor countries. The library, which is open to individual researchers, contains publications from most Third World countries and is an official UN depository. The Annual Report and an IDS publications catalogue available. University of Sussex, Brighton BN1 9RE.

Overseas Development Administration (ODA). ODA is responsible for the management of the British Government's aid programme to developing countries. Official reports and annual statistics are available from HMSO. A list of publications and other material, and a film catalogue, are available free, and the library is open on weekdays. Information Department, ODA, Eland House, Stag Place, London SW1E 5DH.

Overseas Development Institute (ODI). Independent research organisation set up to provide a centre for research in development problems. Free publications list available. Library open on weekdays: enquiries and visitors welcome. 10–11 Percy Street, London W1P 0JB.

Oxfam. Independent voluntary organisation campaigning to involve as many people as possible in the cause of world development and to raise funds for relief and development projects. Free and on sale publications, posters and films. Catalogue. 274 Banbury Road, Oxford OX2 7DZ.

Returned Volunteer Action (RVA). Independent United Kingdom association of ex-overseas volunteers, together with those who support its aims. Access is offered through its clearing house to people who have worked in the Third World – for consultation, seminars and involvement with Third World and development issues; critical information on volunteering; and the distribution of some relevant publications. 1c Cambridge Terrace, Regent's Park, London NW1 4JI.

The Save the Children Fund. Independent voluntary organisation concerned with the welfare of children throughout the world, particularly in the developing countries. Publications and posters about its organisation, the health and education of children in developing countries and its work in disaster areas, slides and films. 157 Clapham Road, London SW9 0PT.

The School of Oriental and African Studies (SOAS). The Extra-Mural Department includes an excellent teachers' resources library, and arranges specialist lectures and conferences on a wide variety of topics connected with the Third World. SOAS, Gower Street, London WC1.

The Shaftesbury Project. The Shaftesbury Project is an initiative by evangelical Christians to consider the implications of involvement in society and to provide a biblical understanding of social and political action. As well as a study group working in the area of Overseas Aid and Development, the Project also has study groups engaged in political action, race relations, crime and punishment, the environment, work and leisure, the role of women etc. It organises conferences and seminars for Christians concerned for informed thinking and action in these fields, and also publishes booklets, papers, study guides, etc., to further these aims. Information can be obtained from The Director, The Shaftesbury Project, 8 Oxford Street, Nottingham NG1 5BH.

Tear Fund (The Evangelical Alliance Relief Fund). Tear Fund is an inter-denominational evangelical relief and development agency working through missionaries and national Christian leaders. In addition to the support of projects and personnel overseas, it runs a child-sponsorship programme, and has set up a subsidiary company, Tearcraft, to import and market handicrafts from developing countries. Educational literature for all ages is published, together with audio-visual aids and publicity material. Free catalogue. 11 Station Road, Teddington, Middlesex TW11 9AJ.

Third World First (3W1). Independent voluntary movement of students and other young people, encouraging action and understanding on the causes of poverty and underdevelopment. Publications include catalogues of Third World music and films available in the United Kingdom, posters, a fund-raising pack and an activists' handbook. Catalogue free, SAE if possible. 232 Cowley Road, Oxford, OX4 1UH.

Third World Publications Ltd. (TWP). TWP, a non-profit making company, distributes books from and about the Third World. It has stocks of development literature published both in Britain and overseas, as well as imports of African, Indian and Caribbean books, and books on theology. Free catalogue. 151 Stratford Road, Birmingham BL1 1RD.

United Nations Children's Fund (UNICEF). UNICEF is financed entirely by voluntary contributions. It is now mainly concerned with long term development programmes meeting the basic needs of children. Free catalogue. United Kingdom Committee for UNICEF, 46–8 Osnaburgh Street, London NW1 3PU.

Voluntary Service Overseas (VSO). VSO is responsible for sending 1,500 volunteers to the Third World in order to work in a wide variety of projects and in many countries. Recruits teachers, librarians, engineers, nurses, laboratory assistants, social workers etc., and liases with Third World Governments in placing these volunteers. VSO does send a considerable number of volunteers to mission institutions, although not in itself a specifically Christian organisation. 9 Belgrave Square, London SW1 8PW. Tel: 01 235 5191.

War on Want. Independent voluntary organisation to inform the British public about poverty, aid and development in the Third World. Free and on sale publications, posters and films. Publications list. 467 Caledonian Road, London N7 9BE.

World Development Movement (WDM). The World Development Movement is an independent voluntary organisation of local action groups concerned to campaign on the political issues of aid and development, and engaged in public education in Britain and other industrialised countries. Both free and for sale publications and posters relating to these campaigns are available from its London office, and a catalogue is available free. The organisation welcomes inquiries. 26 Bedford Chambers, Covent Garden, London WC2E 8HA.

Notes

CHAPTER ONE
(Pages 9 – 17)

1. *First United Kingdom Church Growth Consultation Statistical Survey.*
2. The numbers game is a dangerous one, because the rules are so often changed. Also, as West Indian and Asian communities settle in this country and have families, the problem of how to classify the children of the original post-war immigrants to Britain becomes an increasingly difficult one. Moreover, census returns (1961 and 1971) have not hitherto collected any information directly concerned with race or colour, although the 1981 census did ask a question about ethnic group. And what about the children of mixed marriages? Any statistical information is bound to be tentative, therefore, and subject to more than one possible interpretation. The 1971 census indicated that there were 1,157,170 people living in Britain who were born in the New Commonwealth. This figure represents approximately 60% of the total, the other 40% having been born in the United Kingdom. Thus a fair estimate of the number of Asian and black people living in Britain in 1971 would be 1,975,000. Of these 770,000 have their cultural roots in Asia (India, Pakistan and Bangladesh), 510,000 in the Caribbean, 122,000 in Cyprus, 300,000 in Africa and 272,500 in other countries in the New Commonwealth. But it must again be emphasised that at least 40% of these were born in this country, and are increasingly looking to Britain for a culture, opportunities for employment and all the rights of citizenship that they properly deserve.

   The 1981 census figures were not available at the time of going to press, but they would not differ significantly from those quoted above, because government legislation in the seventies has virtually stopped newcomers to Britain from the New Commonwealth.
3. R. Sider, *Rich Christians in an Age of Hunger – a Biblical Study* Hodder & Stoughton 1978).

CHAPTER TWO
(Pages 18 – 52)

1. James Kirkman, *Unscrambling an Empire* (Chatto & Windus 1966).
2. Robert McNamara, *One Hundred Countries, Two Billion People* (Praeger 1973).
3. Griffin & Enos, *Planning Development* (Addison-Wesley 1970).
4. S. Mooneyham, *What do you say to a hungry World?* (Word Books Texas), quoted in *Rich Christians in an Age of Hunger.*
5. Allowing for population explosion the *average* annual growth rate, measured on a per capita income basis, for the Third World is 3.4%.
6. Hans Singer, *International Development: Growth and Change* (McGraw Hill 1964).
7. Those interested in reading a detailed critical study of this experiment are recommended to read *The Death of the Green Revolution* (N. London Haslemere Group), c/o 515 Liverpool Road, London N7 8NS.
8. Dudley Seers, 'A NEW Look at the Third World Classification' *IDS Bulletin* Vol. 7 No. 4.
9. Geoffrey Lean, *Rich World, Poor World* (Allen & Unwin 1978).
10. Dudley Seers, *op. cit.*

CHAPTER THREE
(Pages 53 – 83)

1. Readers are recommended to read P. Sookhdeo, *All one in Christ Jesus?* (Marshall Morgan & Scott), for a fuller consideration of this area of mission. See also *Guidelines on Dialogue* (World Council of Churches 1979).
2. *UK Protestant Mission Handbook,* Vol. 1 1977 (EMA).

CHAPTER FIVE
(Pages 105 – 132)

1. See M. Hobbs, *Teaching in a Multi-Racial Society* (Association of Christian Teachers 1976).
2. See D. Killingray, *A Plague of Europeans* (Penguin Educational 1972), now unfortunately out of print, but often available in school or college libraries.
3. Interested readers may like to borrow the soundstrip *Time for Change* made by the author, and available on loan from the AVA Unit, Avery Hill College, Bexley Road, Eltham, London SE9.
4. Kenneth Howkins *in Jesus Christ, the Only Way* ed. P. Sookhdeo (Paternoster 1978), p.73.
5. It should be pointed out that this figure represents official central government aid, and obviously does not include the very consider-

able contributions to a wide variety of Third World causes made by the major Third World charities like Oxfam, Christian Aid, Tear Fund and all the others. But the British government's aid figure is the third lowest of all the countries in the EEC – not a statistic of which we can be proud. It should also be noted in this context that the word 'aid' is gradually being replaced by the phrase 'official development assistance' (ODA) as a more accurate description of British Government aid. More to the point, the Overseas Development Administration is necessarily anxious to link *aid* to *trade* and looks for projects where British investment is being used in an aid scheme, and often helps such schemes by means of an additional grant.

6. See appendix for a list of useful addresses to help the interested teacher.
7. See *Hard Questions for Rich Christians* and the *Crusade* study guides listed on page 134.